Cooking for One

The Family Circle® Promise of Success

Welcome to the world of Confident Cooking,
created for you in the Australian **Family Circle®
Test Kitchen,** where recipes are double-tested by
our team of home economists to achieve a
high standard of success—and delicious
results every time.

MURDOCH BOOKS®

Sydney • London • Vancouver • New York

CONTE

Coconut noodles with roast pumpkin, carrot and zucchini, page 49

Prawn and mango salad, page 22

Cottage mushroom soup, page 8

Roasted tomato, feta and rocket pasta, page 33

Vegetarian lasagne, page 90

Pork with herbs and prosciutto, page 51

The Publisher thanks the following for their assistance: Chief Australia; Sunbeam Corporation Ltd; Kambrook; Sheldon & Hammond; Bertoli Olive Oil; Southcorp Appliances.
Front cover: Thai-style chicken and basil stir-fry, page 72
Inside front cover: Lemon lamb kebabs, page 44
Back cover: Blackberry and raspberry parfait, page 104

All recipes are double-tested by our team of home economists. When we test our recipes, we rate them for ease of preparation. The following cookery ratings are on the recipes in this book, making them easy to use and understand.

A single Cooking with Confidence symbol indicates a recipe that is simple and generally quick to make—perfect for beginners.

Two symbols indicate the need for just a little more care and a little more time.

Three symbols indicate special dishes that need more investment in time, care and patience—but the results are worth it.

IMPORTANT
Those who might be at risk from the effects of salmonella food poisoning (the elderly, pregnant women, young children and those suffering from immune deficiency diseases) should consult their GP with any concerns about eating raw eggs.

Fluffy pancakes with blueberry citrus sauce, page 102

Beef and pineapple curry, page 79

LEARNING TO COOK FOR YOURSELF

When faced with preparing a meal for one, many people are tempted to think 'why bother' and just make do with takeaway food or baked beans on toast. However, whether you live on your own or have different eating habits to the rest of your household, it's really quite easy to cook delicious, healthy meals for yourself.

SIZE DOES MATTER

The recipes in this book have been developed to serve one person. The portions will be suitable for most people, however, if you are, say, a professional rugby player or are otherwise physically very active, chances are you are going to have to increase the size of some of the recipes. Similarly, if you lead a sedentary life without much physical activity, some portions may seem a bit overwhelming and you may want to cut them down.

SHOPPING FOR ONE

One of the most difficult aspects of cooking only one serve is knowing how much to buy. If you are adjusting to cooking for one, or even two, it can be particularly difficult to break the habit of filling up the refrigerator with enough food for an entire family.

It can also be difficult to get the proportions right, especially when you are trying to cook a meal for one from a recipe that serves four. If you divide the recipe, you can find yourself faced with problems such as what exactly you are supposed to do with the leftover half can of chopped tomatoes. It can also be difficult to adjust the cooking times of recipes when you alter the ingredients.

COOKING TO FREEZE

Most people these days lead a busy life and don't always have enough time or energy to cook a meal every night. If this sounds familiar, take a look at our Cooking to Freeze section (page 86). Here we have developed larger recipes that can be divided into readily freezable portions. They can be stored in the freezer for up to 3 months and simply taken out and reheated when you want them.

WHAT A WASTE!

It is frustrating but true that there are some ingredients that can't be bought in small, convenient portions. Don't let this put you off, as you can usually freeze any leftovers for later use. Obviously it is essential that you get into the habit of labelling and dating anything you freeze. After all, everything looks the same after a month or two in the freezer and remember, unless you actually use your leftovers you're not saving anything, you're really just delaying throwing them away!

We have done our best to make sure our recipes don't leave you with a refrigerator full of impossible-to-use leftovers. Here are some tips on saving everyday leftovers:

Tomato paste—Freeze in ice cube trays and, once frozen, keep in a freezer bag. Use 1–2 cubes in your recipes as desired. No need to defrost.
Herbs—Chop and measure any leftover fresh herbs into 1 tablespoon portions, wrap in plastic wrap and freeze. Add to curries and stir-fries when needed. Make sure you label which herb it is as they all look similar when chopped and frozen.

Stock—We all know that homemade stock is the best, but let's face it, most of us don't really have the time or the inclination to make our own. Ready-made stocks can be bought at butchers, chicken shops and good delicatessans and are generally much better quality than stock cubes. If there is any leftover stock, pour it into a freezer bag in a measuring jug and measure 1 cup (250 ml). Tie the bag securely and freeze. Once frozen, remove the bag from the jug.
Citrus rind—Grate the rind from lemons, limes and oranges, wrap tightly in plastic wrap in measured teaspoons and freeze. This way you have a ready supply on hand.
Spices—Once opened, packets of spices will stay fresher longer if sealed tightly and kept in the freezer.
Ginger— Pieces of fresh ginger freeze especially well if wrapped tightly in plastic wrap. If you grate frozen ginger, the skin simply folds away as you grate, or you can defrost, peel and use the ginger as the recipe requires. Alternately, peel and thinly slice fresh ginger and keep preserved in a jar of sherry in the fridge. This is great to use in stir-fries along with the ginger-flavoured sherry.
Breadcrumbs—When making fresh breadcrumbs (putting slices of day-old bread through a food processor), make more than you need. Measure the extra crumbs and freeze them in snap-lock freezer bags.
Fruit—Seasonal fruit, such as mango, can be frozen when cheap and plentiful to use at a later date when it is unavailable.

ESSENTIAL INGREDIENTS TO KEEP IN YOUR PANTRY

1 eggs	**6** canned corn kernels	**11** soy sauce	**16** chicken stock cubes
2 canned tomatoes	**7** long-grain rice	**12** couscous	**17** olive oil
3 caster sugar	**8** coconut cream	**13** chicken stock	**18** sweet chilli sauce
4 dried fettucine	**9** wholegrain mustard	**14** rice vermicelli noodles	**19** dried egg noodles
5 red wine vinegar	**10** paprika	**15** soft brown sugar	**20** plain flour

Mushrooms—No, you can't freeze these, but they will last longer without drying out or going slimy if you put them in a paper bag and then in a plastic bag.

Cheese—Parmesan cheese can be kept, already grated, in the freezer to prevent it going mouldy and smelly in the fridge. Place in a freezer bag and remove any air to prevent ice crystals.

REDUCING FAT INTAKE

If you are concerned about your fat intake, there are some simple steps you can take when cooking most recipes to cut down on the fat content. For example, use cooking oil spray and non-stick frying pans when pan-frying food. Use low- or reduced-fat dairy foods instead of the full-cream

varieties. You can even buy light coconut milk in most supermarkets to use as a substitute for the fat-laden coconut milk found in so many curries.

It is a good idea to trim any visible fat from meat before cooking. Chicken is lower in fat if you remove the skin. Chicken breast fillets are very low in fat and can be substituted for other cuts of chicken in most dishes.

SOUPS AND LIGHT MEALS

THAI-STYLE CHICKEN AND CORN SOUP

Preparation time: 10 minutes
Total cooking time: 5 minutes
Serves 1

130 g can corn kernels, undrained
2 small chicken stock cubes, crumbled
2 spring onions, sliced
1 teaspoon finely chopped fresh ginger
125 g chicken tenderloin (or breast fillet), finely sliced
1 teaspoon sweet chilli sauce
1 teaspoon fish sauce
30 g rice vermicelli noodles
2 tablespoons chopped fresh coriander leaves
1/2 teaspoon grated lime rind
2 teaspoons lime juice

1 Bring 2 cups (500 ml) water to the boil in a large saucepan over high heat. Add the corn kernels and their juice, stock cubes, spring onion and ginger, then reduce the heat and simmer for 1 minute.
2 Add the chicken, sweet chilli sauce and fish sauce and simmer for 3 minutes, or until the chicken is cooked through.
3 Meanwhile, place the noodles in a small heatproof bowl and pour in enough boiling water to cover. Leave for 4 minutes, or until softened. Drain the noodles and cut them into short lengths.
4 Add the noodles, coriander, lime rind and lime juice to the soup and serve immediately.

NUTRITION PER SERVE
Protein 33 g; Fat 5 g; Carbohydrate 35 g; Dietary Fibre 5.8 g; Cholesterol 63 mg; 1327 kJ (317 cal)

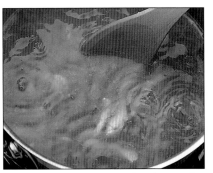

Add the corn kernels, stock cubes, spring onion and ginger to the saucepan.

Place the noodles in a heatproof bowl and cover with boiling water.

COTTAGE MUSHROOM SOUP

Preparation time: 10 minutes
Total cooking time: 10 minutes
Serves 1

25 g butter
2 spring onions, finely chopped
1 small clove garlic, crushed
3 teaspoons plain flour
1¹/2 cups (375 ml) chicken stock
1 large (100 g) field mushroom,
    finely chopped
2 teaspoons chopped fresh
    flat-leaf parsley

1 Heat the butter in a saucepan over medium heat, add the spring onion and garlic and cook for 2–3 minutes, or until the onion is soft. Add the flour and stir for 1 minute, or until the flour is slightly golden.

2 Remove the saucepan from the heat and gradually stir in the chicken stock. Return to the heat, stir through the mushroom and parsley, and bring to the boil, stirring constantly until thickened. Reduce the heat and simmer, covered, for 5 minutes. Season with salt and pepper and serve with fresh crusty French bread.

NUTRITION PER SERVE
Protein 6 g; Fat 22 g; Carbohydrate 11 g; Dietary Fibre 4 g; Cholesterol 65 mg; 1077 kJ (257 cal)

Add the flour to the onion and garlic and cook for 1 minute.

Add the chicken stock, mushroom and parsley and bring to the boil.

CHICKPEA, ROASTED TOMATO AND GARLIC SOUP

Preparation time: 10 minutes
Total cooking time: 30 minutes
Serves 1

2 Roma tomatoes, halved
    lengthways
2 cloves garlic
1/2 teaspoon dried oregano
2 teaspoons olive oil
1 small onion, finely sliced

1 teaspoon tomato paste
1 cup (250 ml) chicken stock
30 g canned chickpeas, rinsed
    and drained

1 Preheat the oven to moderately hot 200°C (400°F/Gas 6). Place the tomato and garlic on a non-stick baking tray. Sprinkle with the dried oregano and some salt and bake for 20 minutes, or until the tomato is soft.
2 Remove the tomato and garlic from the oven. Peel the garlic and place in a food processor or blender with the tomato and process until smooth.

3 Heat the oil in a saucepan, add the onion and cook over low heat for 5 minutes, or until soft. Add the tomato paste and cook for a further 1 minute. Add the stock, tomato mixture and chickpeas. Bring to the boil, then reduce the heat and simmer for 1 minute. Season well with salt and freshly ground black pepper and serve with crusty bread.

NUTRITION PER SERVE
Protein 6 g; Fat 9.5 g; Carbohydrate 13 g; Dietary Fibre 6 g; Cholesterol 22 mg; 981 kJ (234 cal)

Sprinkle oregano and salt over the tomato and garlic and cook for 20 minutes.

Cook the onion in a saucepan over low heat for 5 minutes, or until soft.

Bring the mixture to the boil, then reduce the heat and simmer for 1 minute.

9

CARROT, SPINACH AND COCONUT SOUP

Preparation time: 15 minutes
Total cooking time: 10 minutes
Serves 1

1 large (150 g) carrot, thinly
   sliced
1 medium onion, sliced
1 clove garlic, peeled
1³/4 cups (440 ml) vegetable
   stock
2 tablespoons coconut
   cream
1 teaspoon lime juice
20 g baby English spinach
   leaves
1/4 cup (5 g) fresh coriander
   leaves
1 tablespoon toasted flaked
   coconut

1 Place the carrot, onion, garlic and stock in a saucepan, bring to the boil and cook, covered, for 5 minutes, or until the carrot is very soft.
2 Remove the garlic, pour the mixture into a blender or food processor and blend until smooth.
3 Return the soup to the pan and gently reheat over low heat. Add the coconut cream and stir until well combined. Then add the lime juice and spinach and stir until the spinach has just wilted.
4 Serve immediately, topped with the coriander leaves and toasted flaked coconut.

NUTRITION PER SERVE
Protein 5.5 g; Fat 13 g; Carbohydrate 16 g; Dietary Fibre 8.5 g; Cholesterol 0.5 mg; 850 kJ (205 cal)

Place the carrot, onion, garlic and vegetable stock in a saucepan.

Pour the mixture into a blender or food processor and blend until smooth.

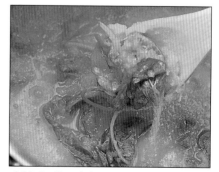

Add the lime juice and spinach and and stir until the spinach has wilted.

Using a sharp knife, cut the chicken tenderloin into bite-size pieces.

Add the garlic and laksa paste to the saucepan and stir-fry for 2 minutes.

Add the chicken pieces to the saucepan and simmer for 5 minutes.

Spoon the chicken mixture over the drained noodles.

EASY CHICKEN LAKSA

Preparation time: 10 minutes
Total cooking time: 10 minutes
Serves 1

50 g rice vermicelli noodles
2 teaspoons peanut oil
1 clove garlic, crushed
2 tablespoons laksa paste
140 g can coconut milk
200 ml chicken stock
125 g chicken tenderloin, cut into bite-size pieces
3 spring onions, cut into 4 cm lengths
8 snow peas, halved on the diagonal
1 tablespoon fresh coriander leaves
50 g fried tofu puffs
1/4 cup (25 g) bean sprouts

fresh coriander leaves, extra, to garnish

1 Put the rice noodles in a heatproof bowl, cover with boiling water and leave for 5 minutes.
2 Heat the oil in a saucepan, add the garlic and laksa paste and stir-fry over medium heat for 2 minutes, or until fragrant.
3 Stir in the coconut milk, chicken stock and 200 ml water, and bring to the boil. Add the chicken, reduce the heat and simmer for 5 minutes, or until the chicken is tender.
4 Add the spring onion and snow peas, and then stir through the coriander leaves.
5 Drain the noodles and place in a warm serving bowl. Spoon in the chicken mixture and top with the tofu puffs, bean sprouts and extra coriander leaves.

NUTRITION PER SERVE
Protein 40 g; Fat 48 g; Carbohydrate 24 g; Dietary Fibre 6.5 g; Cholesterol 67 mg; 2883 kJ (686 cal)

SPINACH AND PEA SOUP

Preparation time: 15 minutes
Total cooking time: 10 minutes
Serves 1

20 g butter
6 spring onions, finely chopped
2 cups (500 ml) chicken stock
1 cup (155 g) frozen peas
2 cups (100 g) English spinach leaves, shredded
1 tablespoon plain yoghurt

1 Heat the butter in a saucepan, add the spring onion and cook over medium heat for 3–4 minutes, or until soft. Add the chicken stock and bring to the boil.

2 Add the peas and spinach and cook for 5 minutes, or until the peas are soft. Cool slightly, place in a blender or food processor and blend until smooth. Place in a warm serving bowl and serve with a swirl of plain yoghurt. Season with freshly ground black pepper.

NUTRITION PER SERVE
Protein 15 g; Fat 19 g; Carbohydrate 16 g; Dietary Fibre 15 g; Cholesterol 55 mg; 1228 kJ (293 cal)

Cook the spring onion in the butter for 3–4 minutes, or until soft.

Add the peas and English spinach to the saucepan and cook for 5 minutes.

Pour the mixture into a food processor or blender and blend until smooth.

CURRIED ORANGE SWEET POTATO AND APPLE SOUP

Preparation time: 10 minutes
Total cooking time: 15 minutes
Serves 1

1 teaspoon oil
1 small onion, chopped
1/4 teaspoon Madras curry powder
200 g orange sweet potato,
    peeled and chopped
1 small green apple, peeled and
    chopped
1 cup (250 ml) chicken or
    vegetable stock

1 Heat the oil in a saucepan, add the onion and curry powder and cook over medium heat for 3 minutes, or until the onion is soft.
2 Add the sweet potato, apple and stock to the pan. Bring to the boil, then reduce the heat and simmer, covered, for 10 minutes, or until the sweet potato is soft.

3 Remove from the heat, place in a blender or food processor and blend until smooth. Return to the pan and gently reheat. Season with salt and pepper and serve with crusty bread.

NUTRITION PER SERVE
Protein 5 g; Fat 6 g; Carbohydrate 52 g; Dietary Fibre 7.5 g; Cholesterol 0.5 mg; 1175 kJ (280 cal)

C O O K ' S   F I L E

Note: Always fry off the curry powder to avoid a raw spice taste.

Cook the onion and curry powder in a saucepan over medium heat for 3 minutes.

Simmer for 10 minutes, or until the orange sweet potato is soft.

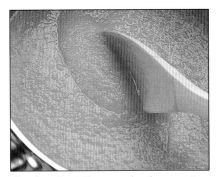

Gently reheat the soup in the saucepan before serving.

POACHED SALMON IN GINGER BROTH

Preparation time: 5 minutes
Total cooking time: 15 minutes
Serves 1

2 teaspoons oil
2 spring onions, sliced on the
    diagonal
2 teaspoons finely chopped
    fresh ginger
1 tablespoon fish sauce
1 tablespoon soft brown sugar
200 g salmon fillet or cutlet
2 teaspoons lime juice
$^1/_3$ cup (40 g) frozen baby peas
6 fresh coriander leaves

1 Heat the oil in a frying pan, add the spring onion and chopped ginger and cook, stirring, over medium heat for 2 minutes.

2 Add the fish sauce, soft brown sugar and 1$^1/_4$ cups (315 ml) water and bring to the boil. Reduce the heat to low, add the salmon and cook for 3 minutes. Turn over and cook for a further minute, or until the salmon is just cooked. Place the salmon in a warm, shallow serving bowl, cover with foil and keep warm. Boil the liquid in the pan for 3–5 minutes, or until it has reduced by half. Add the lime juice.

3 Meanwhile, bring a small saucepan of water to the boil, add the peas and cook for 1 minute, or until tender. Drain. Spoon the peas around the salmon, ladle the broth over the top and scatter with the coriander leaves.

NUTRITION PER SERVE
Protein 20 g; Fat 22 g; Carbohydrate 25 g; Dietary Fibre 4 g; Cholesterol 70 mg; 1612 kJ (384 cal)

Add the spring onion and ginger to the frying pan and cook for 2 minutes.

Poach the fish for 3 minutes on one side, turn over and poach for another minute.

Bring the liquid to the boil and boil until it has reduced by half.

BAKED EGGS ITALIAN STYLE

Preparation time: 10 minutes
Total cooking time: 20 minutes
Serves 1

Prosciutto toasts
1 long white bread roll
3 teaspoons olive oil
2 thin slices prosciutto

2 eggs, at room temperature
1 tomato, halved, seeded and
    finely chopped
1 teaspoon snipped fresh chives

2 teaspoons shredded fresh
    basil
3 pitted black olives, finely
    chopped
1 teaspoon extra virgin olive oil
2 tablespoons grated Parmesan

1 Preheat the oven to moderately hot 200°C (400°F/Gas 6). Lightly grease a ³/4 cup (185 ml) ovenproof dish.
2 To make the prosciutto toasts, remove the crusts and slice the roll lengthways into two slices. Brush the bread on both sides with the oil and arrange the prosciutto on top of each slice. Set aside until ready to use.
3 Break the eggs into the prepared

dish. Place the tomato, chives, basil, olives and olive oil in a separate bowl and season with salt and pepper. Mix together well and spoon over the eggs. Sprinkle the Parmesan over the top, place the dish on a baking tray and bake for 5 minutes. Arrange the prosciutto toasts alongside and bake for a further 10–15 minutes, or until the eggs are just set and the prosciutto toasts are crisp. Slice the toasts in half and serve immediately.

NUTRITION PER SERVE
Protein 32 g; Fat 37 g; Carbohydrate 47 g; Dietary Fibre 5 g; Cholesterol 384 mg; 2726 kJ (650 cal)

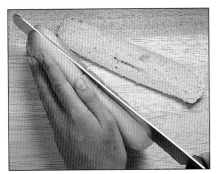

Remove the crusts, then slice the bread roll lengthways into two slices.

Spoon the combined tomato, chives, basil, olives and olive oil over the eggs.

Bake the eggs and toasts in a moderately hot oven until the eggs are set.

CRAB CAKES

Preparation time: 15 minutes
Total cooking time: 6 minutes
Serves 1

170 g can crabmeat, drained,
   liquid reserved
1 egg, lightly beaten
1/4 cup (35 g) finely chopped
   celery
1 spring onion, finely chopped
1 tablespoon chopped fresh
   coriander leaves
1/4 cup (25 g) dry breadcrumbs
1–2 drops Tabasco sauce,
   to taste
1 tablespoon light olive oil

Sesame mayonnaise
2 tablespoons whole-egg
   mayonnaise
2 teaspoons toasted sesame
   seeds (see Note)
1 teaspoon sweet chilli sauce
1/2 teaspoon grated fresh ginger
1/4 teaspoon soy sauce

1 Squeeze the crab meat dry and place in a bowl with 2 teaspoons of the liquid and the egg, celery, spring onion, coriander, breadcrumbs and Tabasco. Mix together and season, then cover and leave for 5 minutes. Divide the mixture into 3 portions, shape into patties and flatten slightly.
2 Heat the oil in a non-stick frying pan, add the crab cakes and cook over medium heat for 2–3 minutes on each side, or until golden brown and cooked through. Drain well.
3 To make the sesame mayonnaise, place all the ingredients in a small bowl and mix well. Spoon over the crab cakes and serve with a salad.

NUTRITION PER SERVE
Protein 33 g; Fat 40 g; Carbohydrate 29 g; Dietary Fibre 3 g; Cholesterol 335 mg; 2565 kJ (613 cal)

COOK'S FILE

Note: If you want to reduce the fat content in this recipe, try substituting low-fat yoghurt for the mayonnaise.

Place the crab cake ingredients in a bowl and mix together well.

Divide the mixture into 3 even portions and shape into patties.

Cook the crab cakes for 2–3 minutes on each side, or until golden brown.

ASIAN OMELETTE

Preparation time: 5 minutes
Total cooking time: 10 minutes
Serves 1

2 teaspoons soy sauce
2 teaspoons kecap manis
2 teaspoons dry sherry
1 tablespoon peanut oil
2 spring onions, sliced on the
   diagonal
1 teaspoon grated fresh ginger
125 g button mushrooms, sliced
3 eggs, lightly beaten
1 tablespoon chopped fresh
   coriander leaves

1 Put the soy sauce, kecap manis and sherry in a small bowl and mix well. Heat half the peanut oil in a saucepan, add the spring onion and ginger, and cook over low heat for 3–4 minutes, or until the onion is soft but not brown. Add the soy sauce mixture and the mushrooms and stir over medium heat for 3 minutes, or until the mushrooms are soft. Keep warm.

2 Combine the lightly beaten eggs with 1 tablespoon water in a small bowl and season with salt and pepper. Heat the remaining peanut oil in a small non-stick frying pan, add the beaten eggs and cook over medium heat for 2–3 minutes, or until just set.

3 Spoon the warm mushroom mixture onto one half of the omelette and top with half the chopped coriander leaves. Fold the omelette over and gently slide onto a warm plate. Top with the remaining coriander leaves. Serve immediately with a green salad.

NUTRITION PER SERVE
Protein 24 g; Fat 35 g; Carbohydrate 4.5 g; Dietary Fibre 4 g; Cholesterol 540 mg; 1780 kJ (425 cal)

COOK'S FILE

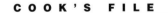

Variation: Fresh shiitake or oyster mushrooms can be used instead of button mushrooms. For a heartier meal, try adding some chopped cooked barbecue pork.

Add the soy mixture and the mushrooms to the saucepan and stir for 3 minutes.

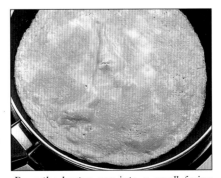

Pour the beaten egg into a small frying pan and cook until lightly set.

Add the warm mushroom mixture to the omelette and top with half the coriander.

ROCKET AND RICOTTA MUSHROOMS

Preparation time: 10 minutes
Total cooking time: 5 minutes
Serves 1

60 g rocket leaves
1/2 cup (125 g) low-fat ricotta
1 egg yolk
1 tablespoon snipped fresh
   chives
20 g butter, melted
2 cloves garlic, crushed
2 large flat field mushrooms,
   stalks removed

2 tablespoons freshly grated
   Parmesan
rocket leaves, extra, to serve

1 Put the rocket in a colander over a bowl and pour boiling water over it until just wilted. Run cold water over the rocket until it is cool enough to touch and squeeze out as much liquid as possible, then roughly chop.
2 Place the ricotta in a bowl, add the egg yolk, chives and rocket, and mix together well. Season to taste with salt and freshly ground black pepper.
3 Combine the butter and garlic and brush over the mushrooms. Place flat-side-down on a non-stick grill tray and cook under high heat for 1 minute.

4 Divide the ricotta mixture between the mushrooms and smooth the surface. Sprinkle with the Parmesan and grill for 3 minutes, or until the cheese is golden brown. Serve with the extra rocket.

NUTRITION PER SERVE
Protein 25 g; Fat 38 g; Carbohydrate 3.5 g; Dietary Fibre 4 g; Cholesterol 300 mg; 1897 kJ (455 cal)

COOK'S FILE

Serving suggestion: Serve with a salad of sliced tomatoes sprinkled with shredded fresh basil and toasted pine nuts, drizzled with extra virgin olive oil and balsamic vinegar.

Add the egg yolk, chives and rocket to the ricotta and mix well.

Place the mushrooms flat-side-down on a non-stick grill tray and cook for 1 minute.

Divide the ricotta mixture evenly between the mushrooms and grill for 3 minutes.

FETTUCINE WITH BROAD BEANS AND HALOUMI

Preparation time: 15 minutes
Total cooking time: 12 minutes
Serves 1

100 g fettucine
1 tablespoon lemon juice
1 tablespoon olive oil
2 teaspoons chopped fresh
   basil
40 g broad beans (fresh or
   frozen)
100 g haloumi cheese, sliced
   lengthways into thin slices
2 Roma tomatoes, cut into
   quarters
olive oil, extra, for brushing
fresh basil leaves, to garnish

1 Bring a large saucepan of salted water to the boil and cook the fettucine until *al dente*. Drain and place in a bowl.
2 Combine the lemon juice, olive oil and basil in a small jug and pour over the cooked fettucine. Season with salt and pepper and toss to coat.
3 Place the broad beans in boiling water for 30 seconds, then drain and rinse under cold running water. Peel off the outer skins.
4 Brush the haloumi and tomato with the extra olive oil. Place on a char-grill plate over high heat and cook for 30 seconds each side, or until starting to brown.
5 To serve, toss the tomato and broad beans through the fettucine. Arrange the haloumi and basil leaves over the top and season with salt and pepper.

Slice the haloumi cheese lengthways into thin slices.

Pour the combined lemon juice, olive oil and basil over the cooked fettucine.

Blanch the beans in boiling water for 30 seconds and peel off the outer skins.

Cook the haloumi and tomato slices on a char-grill plate for 30 seconds each side.

NUTRITION PER SERVE
Protein 35 g; Fat 45 g; Carbohydrate 75 g; Dietary Fibre 8.5 g; Cholesterol 53 mg; 3642 kJ (870 cal)

QUICK SALMON SOUFFLE

Preparation time: 10 minutes
Total cooking time: 30 minutes
Serves 1

1/3 **cup (25 g) fresh breadcrumbs (see Note)**
1/4 **cup (60 ml) cream**
1/2 **teaspoon finely chopped fresh dill**
1 **teaspoon snipped fresh chives**
1 **egg, lightly beaten**
50 **g canned red salmon, drained and finely flaked**
1/4 **teaspoon lemon juice**

1 Preheat the oven to moderately hot 200°C (400°F/Gas 6). Lightly grease a 1 1/4 cup (315 ml) soufflé dish. Combine the breadcrumbs, cream, dill and chives in a bowl and leave to stand for 2 minutes. Add the egg, salmon and lemon juice and mix well. Season.

2 Spoon into the prepared dish and bake for 30 minutes, or until golden and well puffed. Serve immediately.

NUTRITION PER SERVE
Protein 22 g; Fat 37 g; Carbohydrate 18 g; Dietary Fibre 1 g; Cholesterol 295 mg; 2060 kJ (490 cal)

COOK'S FILE

Note: To make 1/3 cup (25 g) fresh breadcrumbs, process 1 slice of bread, crusts removed, in a food processor.

Place the drained red salmon in a bowl and gently flake with a fork.

Add the egg, salmon and lemon juice to the mixture and mix well.

Bake the soufflé for 30 minutes, or until golden and well puffed.

FETA AND TOMATO BRUSCHETTA

Preparation time: 15 minutes
Total cooking time: 7 minutes
Serves 1

60 g ricotta
40 g feta, crumbled
2 teaspoons roughly chopped
    fresh basil leaves
1 large crusty bread roll

2 teaspoons olive oil
1/4 small red onion, finely chopped
110 g cherry tomatoes, halved
4 fresh basil leaves, extra

1 Combine the ricotta, feta and chopped basil in a bowl and season.
2 Slice the roll lengthways into 2 slices, removing the crusts. Place the slices on a grill tray and toast under a hot grill for 1 minute each side, or until golden brown.
3 Heat the oil in a small frying pan, add the onion and cook over medium heat for 3 minutes, or until soft. Add the tomato and extra basil leaves and cook for a further 2 minutes. Season with salt and ground black pepper.
4 To serve, spread the toasts with the cheese mixture and top with the tomato and basil mixture.

NUTRITION PER SERVE
Protein 22 g; Fat 28 g; Carbohydrate 40 g; Dietary Fibre 4.6 g; Cholesterol 55 mg; 2098 kJ (500 cal)

Place the ricotta, feta and basil in a bowl and mix together well.

Remove the crusts and cut the bread roll into 2 slices.

Add the tomato and basil leaves to the onion and cook for 2 minutes.

PRAWN AND MANGO SALAD

Preparation time: 20 minutes
Total cooking time: nil
Serves 1

2 large iceberg lettuce leaves,
   washed and dried
8 cooked tiger prawns, peeled
   and deveined

½ mango, cut into 2 cm cubes
½ avocado, cut into 2 cm cubes
1 spring onion, thinly sliced on
   the diagonal
1 teaspoon finely shredded
   fresh mint leaves
1 tablespoon lime juice

1 Finely shred one lettuce leaf and place in a bowl with the prawns, mango, avocado, spring onion, mint and lime juice and mix well.

2 Place the prawn mixture in the remaining lettuce leaf and serve.

NUTRITION PER SERVE
Protein 47 g; Fat 29 g; Carbohydrate 12 g; Dietary Fibre 7.5 g; Cholesterol 298 mg; 2078 kJ (495 cal)

COOK'S FILE

Note: For a delicious dressing, mix 1 teaspoon lime juice into 1 tablespoon whole-egg mayonnaise.

Cut down the back of the prawn and remove the intestinal tract.

Combine the prawns with the rest of the salad ingredients.

Spoon the prawn mixture into the remaining lettuce leaf to serve.

POTATO, CARROT AND TUNA CAKES

Preparation time: 15 minutes +
  20 minutes refrigeration
Total cooking time: 20 minutes
Serves 1

200 g potato, cut into large
  wedges
95 g can tuna, drained
1 spring onion, finely chopped
1 small (40 g) carrot, grated
1 tablespoon finely chopped
  fresh flat-leaf parsley

1 teaspoon grated lemon rind
plain flour, for dusting
1 egg, lightly beaten
1/2 cup (50 g) dry breadcrumbs
oil, for shallow-frying

1 Bring a saucepan of lightly salted water to the boil, add the potato and cook for 15 minutes, or until tender. Drain and mash.
2 Place the tuna in a small bowl and flake with a fork. Add the spring onion, mashed potato, carrot, parsley and lemon rind. Mix together well and form into two flat patties.
3 Coat the patties in the flour, shake

off any excess, dip in the egg and then the breadcrumbs. Place the patties on a flat plate, cover and refrigerate for 20 minutes.
4 Heat the oil in a small frying pan to a depth of 1.5 cm. Cook the patties for 2–3 minutes each side, or until golden brown and heated through. Drain on paper towels and serve hot with tartare sauce, lemon wedges and a green salad, if desired.

NUTRITION PER SERVE
Protein 42 g; Fat 29 g; Carbohydrate 65 g; Dietary Fibre 6.5 g; Cholesterol 230 mg; 2878 kJ (687 cal)

Combine the tuna, spring onion, mashed potato, carrot, parsley and lemon rind.

Coat each patty in flour, before dipping in egg and then breadcrumbs.

Cook the patties in a small frying pan for 2–3 minutes each side.

23

CORN FRITTERS AND TOMATO SALSA

Preparation time: 15 minutes +
 10 minutes standing
Total cooking time: 6 minutes
Serves 1

2 teaspoons olive oil
1/4 small onion, finely
 chopped
1 rasher bacon, finely chopped
1/4 cup (30 g) self-raising
 flour
1/3 cup (50 g) polenta
75 g can corn kernels, drained
100 ml milk
1 tablespoon olive oil, extra

Tomato salsa
1 vine-ripened tomato, seeded
 and finely diced
1/4 small Lebanese cucumber,
 seeded and finely diced
2 teaspoons snipped fresh
 chives
2 teaspoons balsamic vinegar

1 Heat the oil in a frying pan, add the onion and bacon and cook over medium heat for 3–4 minutes, or until the onion is soft. Leave to cool.

2 Sift the flour into a bowl and stir through the polenta. Add the bacon mixture and the corn, and mix together well. Add the milk and stir until just combined. Leave for 10 minutes.

3 Heat the extra oil in a large non-stick frying pan. Divide the mixture into three and spoon into the pan to make three corn fritters. Cook over medium heat for 1 minute, or until bubbles appear on the surface and the fritters brown around the edges. Turn the fritters over and cook for a further 30 seconds–1 minute, or until cooked through and golden. Drain on crumpled paper towels.

4 To make the salsa, place the tomato, cucumber, chives and balsamic vinegar in a small bowl and mix together well. Serve immediately with the corn fritters and a green salad.

NUTRITION PER SERVE
Protein 22 g; Fat 37 g; Carbohydrate 80 g; Dietary Fibre 7.5 g; Cholesterol 33 mg; 3070 kJ (735 cal)

Cut the cucumber in half and scrape out the seeds with a teaspoon.

Add the milk to the corn cake mixture and leave for 10 minutes.

Cook the corn cakes for 1 minute on each side, or until cooked through.

Mix together the tomato, cucumber, chives and balsamic vinegar.

CROQUE-MONSIEUR

Preparation time: 10 minutes
Total cooking time: 10 minutes
Serves 1

1 teaspoon oil
2 eggs
4 slices white bread
1 tablespoon Dijon mustard
100 g finely sliced or shaved
   honey-smoked leg ham
50 g shaved Jarlsberg or
   Swiss cheese
15 g butter, softened

1 Heat the oil in a non-stick frying pan, add the eggs one at a time and fry until cooked to your liking. Spread the bread with the Dijon mustard.
2 Top two of the bread slices each with half of the shaved ham, an egg and half the cheese then place the remaining two slices of bread on top. Butter the outside of each slice.
3 Heat a non-stick frying pan, carefully place the sandwiches in the pan, weigh them down with a plate if desired, and cook over medium heat for 2–3 minutes each side, or until they are crisp and golden on both sides and the cheese has melted. Serve immediately.

NUTRITION PER SERVE
Protein 50 g; Fat 47 g; Carbohydrate 28 g; Dietary Fibre 2.5 g; Cholesterol 495 mg; 3100 kJ (740 cal)

COOK'S FILE

Note: This recipe also works well in a jaffle maker.
Variation: Try replacing the ham with cooked chicken to make a croque-madame.

Cook the eggs to your liking in a non-stick frying pan.

Spread the bread with Dijon mustard and top with ham, egg and cheese.

Cook the sandwiches until crisp and golden on both sides.

PASTA AND RICE

ORANGE SWEET POTATO AND PROSCIUTTO PENNE

Preparation time: 10 minutes
Total cooking time: 15 minutes
Serves 1

125 g penne
150 g orange sweet potato,
    cut into 1 cm cubes
1 tablespoon extra virgin
    olive oil
2 spring onions, sliced
1 small clove garlic, crushed
2 thin slices prosciutto, chopped
30 g sun-dried tomatoes in oil,
    drained and sliced
1–2 tablespoons shredded
    fresh basil leaves

1 Bring a large saucepan of salted water to the boil and cook the penne until *al dente*. Drain. Return to the pan.
2 Meanwhile, steam the sweet potato for 5 minutes, or until tender. Heat the oil in a saucepan, add the spring onion, garlic and sweet potato and stir over medium heat for 2–3 minutes, or until the spring onion is soft. Add the prosciutto and tomato and cook for a further 1 minute.
3 Add the sweet potato mixture to the penne and toss over low heat until heated through. Add the basil and season with freshly ground black pepper. Serve immediately with crusty bread and a leafy green salad.

NUTRITION PER SERVE
Protein 20 g; Fat 20 g; Carbohydrate 115 g; Dietary Fibre 11 g; Cholesterol 5 mg; 3065 kJ (732 cal)

COOK'S FILE

Note: Orange sweet potato is also known as kumera.

Cook the spring onion, garlic and sweet potato for 2–3 minutes.

Add the sweet potato mixture to the cooked pasta and heat through.

CREAMY BOSCAIOLA

Preparation time: 10 minutes
Total cooking time: 15 minutes
Serves 1

150 g spaghetti
2 teaspoons oil
1 rasher bacon, chopped
50 g button mushrooms, sliced
1/2 cup (125 ml) cream
1 spring onion, sliced
2 teaspoons chopped fresh
  flat-leaf parsley
grated Parmesan, to serve

1 Bring a large saucepan of salted water to the boil and cook the spaghetti until *al dente*. Drain, return to the pan and keep warm.

2 Meanwhile, heat the oil in a frying pan, add the bacon and mushrooms and cook, stirring, over medium heat for 5 minutes, or until golden brown.

3 Stir in the cream and scrape across the bottom of the pan with a wooden spoon to make sure the mixture is not sticking. Bring to the boil and cook over high heat for 5 minutes, or until the sauce is thick enough to coat the back of the spoon.

4 Stir through the spring onion and season with salt and freshly ground black pepper. Pour the sauce over the pasta and toss well. Sprinkle with the chopped parsley and grated Parmesan, if desired. Serve with a green salad and crusty bread.

NUTRITION PER SERVE
Protein 20 g; Fat 67 g; Carbohydrate 109 g; Dietary Fibre 7.5 g; Cholesterol 190 mg; 4767 kJ (1140 cal)

COOK'S FILE

Note: Grated Parmesan will keep fresh if sealed in a freezer bag or airtight container in the freezer.

Cook the bacon and mushrooms in a frying pan until golden brown.

Bring the sauce to the boil and cook until thick enough to coat the back of the spoon.

Pour the boscaiola sauce over the cooked spaghetti and toss to combine.

PESTO PASTA

Preparation time: 10 minutes
Total cooking time: 15 minutes
Serves 1

150 g spaghetti
1 tablespoon pine nuts
2 tablespoons finely grated
    Parmesan
60 g fresh basil leaves

2 small cloves garlic, crushed
1–2 tablespoons olive oil
grated Parmesan, extra,
    to serve

1 Bring a saucepan of salted water to the boil, add the spaghetti and cook until *al dente*. Drain and keep warm.
2 Meanwhile, to make the pesto, toast the pine nuts in a dry frying pan for 2–3 minutes, or until lightly browned. Place in a food processor or blender with the Parmesan, basil and garlic and process until finely chopped. With the motor running, slowly add the oil in a thin stream. Season.
3 Add the pesto to the spaghetti and and toss until well coated. Serve with extra grated Parmesan.

NUTRITION PER SERVE
Protein 30 g; Fat 64 g; Carbohydrate 107 g; Dietary Fibre 9.5 g; Cholesterol 28 mg; 4705 kJ (1125 cal)

Toast the pine nuts in a dry frying pan until lightly browned.

Process the pine nuts, Parmesan, basil and garlic in a food processor.

Add the pesto to the cooked spaghetti and toss well to coat.

RIGATONI WITH CHICKEN AND SUN-DRIED TOMATO CREAM SAUCE

Preparation time: 5 minutes
Total cooking time: 20 minutes
Serves 1

120 g rigatoni
1 teaspoon olive oil
1 chicken breast fillet, thinly
    sliced
1 ripe tomato, diced
50 g sun-dried tomatoes in oil,
    thinly sliced
2 teaspoons sun-dried tomato
    paste (see Note)
10 small fresh basil leaves
100 ml cream
50 ml chicken stock

1 Bring a large saucepan of salted water to the boil and cook the rigatoni until *al dente*. Drain and rinse under running water.

2 Meanwhile, heat the oil in a deep frying pan and cook the chicken over high heat for 4 minutes each side, or until browned and cooked through. Remove from the pan and keep warm.

3 Return the pan to the heat and add the tomato, sun-dried tomato, sun-dried tomato paste and half the basil leaves. Cook over medium heat for 5 minutes, or until the tomato starts to soften. Stir through the cream and chicken stock and bring to the boil, stirring constantly.

4 Reduce the heat and return the chicken to the pan. Add the rigatoni and season with freshly ground black pepper. Heat gently until the chicken and pasta are warmed through. Top with the remaining basil leaves and serve immediately with crusty bread.

NUTRITION PER SERVE
Protein 45 g; Fat 50 g; Carbohydrate 90 g; Dietary Fibre 7.5 g; Cholesterol 195 mg; 4227 kJ (1010 cal)

COOK'S FILE

Note: Sun-dried tomato paste is available in good supermarkets. Or, you can make your own by processing whole sun-dried tomatoes in oil, and a little of their oil, until a smooth paste is formed.

Drain the cooked rigatoni and rinse under running water.

Cook the chicken over high heat until browned and cooked through.

Cook the tomato, sun-dried tomato, sun-dried tomato paste and half the basil.

Return the chicken to the pan and toss through the rigatoni.

SMOKED SALMON PASTA

Preparation time: 10 minutes
Total cooking time: 15 minutes
Serves 1

125 g spiral pasta
1 teaspoon olive oil
1 spring onion, finely chopped
50 g button mushrooms, sliced
1/4 cup (60 ml) dry white
    wine
100 ml cream
2 teaspoons finely chopped
    fresh dill

1 teaspoon lemon juice
1/4 cup (25 g) grated Parmesan
50 g smoked salmon, cut into
    strips
shaved Parmesan, to garnish
lemon wedges, to serve

1 Bring a large saucepan of salted water to the boil, add the pasta and cook until *al dente*. Drain, return to the pan and keep warm.
2 Meanwhile, heat the oil in a small saucepan, add the spring onion and mushrooms and cook over medium heat for 1–2 minutes, or until soft. Add the wine and cream and bring to

the boil, then reduce the heat and simmer for 1 minute.
3 Pour the mushroom sauce over the pasta and stir through the dill and lemon juice. Add the Parmesan and stir until warmed through. Remove from the heat and stir in the smoked salmon. Season with freshly ground black pepper and garnish with the shaved Parmesan. Serve with the lemon wedges.

NUTRITION PER SERVE
Protein 40 g; Fat 60 g; Carbohydrate 90 g; Dietary Fibre 7.8 g; Cholesterol 184 mg; 4608 kJ (1101 cal)

Cook the spring onion and mushrooms over medium heat until soft.

Add the wine and cream to the saucepan and bring to the boil.

Stir the smoked salmon through the pasta to gently warm.

ROASTED PUMPKIN FETTUCINE

Preparation time: 15 minutes
Total cooking time: 45 minutes
Serves 1

500 g pumpkin
olive oil spray
125 g fettucine or ribbon pasta
pinch ground nutmeg
2 tablespoons finely grated
    Parmesan
1/4 cup (60 ml) light cream
1/3 cup (80 ml) chicken stock
1 tablespoon snipped fresh
    chives
1 spring onion, finely chopped

1 Preheat the oven to moderately hot 200°C (400°F/Gas 6). Remove the skin and seeds from the pumpkin and cut into 2 cm pieces. Place the pumpkin pieces in a baking dish and lightly spray with oil. Bake for 45 minutes, or until browned and cooked through. Cool slightly.

2 Meanwhile, bring a large saucepan of salted water to the boil and cook the fettucine until *al dente*, then drain. Return to the pan and keep warm.

3 Place the pumpkin in a food processor or blender with the nutmeg, Parmesan, cream and stock, and process until smooth.

4 Toss the pumpkin mixture through the pasta. Add the chives and spring onion and warm over low heat. Season and serve immediately.

NUTRITION PER SERVE
Protein 35 g; Fat 45 g; Carbohydrate 123 g; Dietary Fibre 13 g; Cholesterol 100 mg; 4359 kJ (1040 cal)

Place the pumpkin pieces in a baking dish and bake until lightly browned.

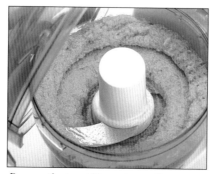

Process the pumpkin, nutmeg, Parmesan, cream and stock until smooth.

Toss the pumpkin mixture through the cooked pasta.

ROASTED TOMATO, FETA AND ROCKET PASTA

Preparation time: 15 minutes
Total cooking time: 1 hour
Serves 1

2 teaspoons olive oil
$1/4$ teaspoon dried oregano
1 clove garlic, finely chopped
2 Roma tomatoes, halved
100 g spaghetti
1 slice prosciutto
4 Kalamata olives
50 g feta, cut into bite-size
    cubes
1 teaspoon balsamic vinegar
$1^1/2$ tablespoons olive oil,
    extra
1 clove garlic, thinly sliced,
    extra
$3/4$ cup (15 g) loosely packed
    rocket leaves, washed
    and trimmed

1 Preheat the oven to slow 150°C (300°F/Gas 2). Combine the olive oil, oregano, garlic and $1/4$ teaspoon salt in a bowl. Add the tomato and toss to combine, rubbing the mixture onto the cut halves of the tomato. Place the tomato cut-side-up on a lined baking tray and cook in the oven for 1 hour.

2 Meanwhile, bring a large saucepan of salted water to the boil and cook the spaghetti until *al dente*. Drain and keep warm. Place the prosciutto on a grill tray and cook under a hot grill, turning once, for 3–4 minutes, or until crispy. Break into pieces.

3 Toss the tomato, olives, feta, spaghetti and balsamic vinegar in a bowl and keep warm.

4 Heat the extra olive oil in a small saucepan and cook the extra garlic over low heat, without burning, for 1–2 minutes, or until the garlic has infused the oil.

5 Pour the garlic and oil over the spaghetti mixture, add the rocket leaves and toss well. Sprinkle with the prosciutto pieces and season with salt and freshly ground black pepper. Serve immediately.

NUTRITION PER SERVE
Protein 14 g; Fat 40 g; Carbohydrate 75 g; Dietary Fibre 9 g; Cholesterol 2.5 mg; 3020 kJ (720 cal)

Rub the olive oil, oregano, garlic and salt mixture into the cut halves of the tomato.

Grill the prosciutto until crispy, then break into small pieces.

Toss the tomato, olives, feta, spaghetti and balsamic vinegar in a bowl.

MACARONI CHEESE WITH CRISPY BACON ROLLS

Preparation time: 10 minutes
Total cooking time: 15 minutes
Serves 1

3/4 cup (115 g) elbow macaroni
15 g butter
3 teaspoons plain flour
3/4 cup (185 ml) milk
70 g grated Cheddar
3 cherry tomatoes, halved
2 rashers bacon

1 Lightly grease a 2 cup (500 ml) ovenproof dish. Bring a large saucepan of salted water to the boil and cook the macaroni until *al dente*. Drain, return to the pan and keep warm.
2 Meanwhile, melt the butter in a small saucepan over medium heat, add the flour and stir constantly for 1 minute. Remove from the heat and gradually stir in the milk. Return to the heat and stir constantly until the sauce boils and thickens. Stir the Cheddar through the sauce. Reduce the heat and simmer for 3 minutes. Season. Stir the pasta through the sauce. Spoon into the prepared dish

and arrange the tomato halves on top.
3 Cut the bacon in half lengthways, roll up and secure with a toothpick. Place the macaroni cheese and bacon rolls on a grill tray and grill under a hot grill, turning the bacon over halfway through, for 5–6 minutes, or until the bacon is crisp and the cheese is golden. Remove the toothpicks and arrange the bacon rolls over the macaroni cheese. Serve immediately.

NUTRITION PER SERVE
Protein 45 g; Fat 46 g; Carbohydrate 100 g; Dietary Fibre 7 g; Cholesterol 150 mg; 4130 kJ (987 cal)

Stir the cooked macaroni through the cheese sauce.

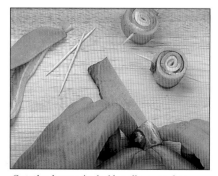

Cut the bacon in half, roll up and secure with a toothpick.

Place under a grill until the bacon is crisp and the cheese is golden.

Cut three pieces from the lasagne sheets to fit the base of the prepared dish.

Drizzle the tomato and mushrooms with the oil and thyme and bake until soft.

Stir the spinach, sour cream and cream into the leek mixture.

Cover with another piece of lasagne and repeat with the remaining mixture.

CREAMY SPINACH AND LEEK LASAGNE

Preparation time: 20 minutes
Total cooking time: 45 minutes
Serves 1

2 fresh lasagne sheets
2 Roma tomatoes, halved
1 (100 g) large field mushroom, stalk removed
1 tablespoon extra virgin olive oil
1 teaspoon finely chopped fresh thyme
20 g butter
1 leek, finely sliced
1 clove garlic, crushed
250 g packet frozen chopped spinach, thawed
¼ cup (60 g) light sour cream
⅓ cup (80 ml) light cream
⅔ cup (160 g) low-fat ricotta
1 egg, lightly beaten
¼ cup (30 g) grated Cheddar

1 Preheat the oven to moderately hot 200°C (400°F/Gas 6). Lightly grease a 2 cup (500 ml) ovenproof dish. Cut three pieces from the lasagne sheets to fit the base of the prepared dish.

2 Place the tomato and mushroom face down in a baking dish. Put the oil and thyme in a bowl, mix together well and drizzle over the tomato and mushroom. Season with salt and pepper. Bake for 15 minutes, then turn over and bake for another 10 minutes, or until softened. Roughly chop.

3 Meanwhile, heat the butter in a frying pan, add the leek and garlic and cook over medium heat for 2–3 minutes, or until soft. Squeeze the liquid from the spinach and add to the leek mixture with the sour cream and cream. Stir well, then bring to the boil and cook for 5 minutes, or until reduced slightly. Stir in the chopped tomato and mushroom.

4 To assemble, place a piece of lasagne in the base of the dish and spoon in half the spinach, leek, tomato and mushroom mixture. Cover with another piece and repeat with the remaining mixture. Spread with the combined ricotta and egg and sprinkle with Cheddar. Place on a baking tray and bake for 20 minutes, or until golden. Serve.

NUTRITION PER SERVE
Protein 58 g; Fat 102 g; Carbohydrate 60 g; Dietary Fibre 23 g; Cholesterol 435 mg; 5833 kJ (1393 cal)

BEEF SAUSAGE PASTA

Preparation time: 10 minutes
Total cooking time: 15 minutes
Serves 1

1/2 cup (40 g) spiral pasta
1 thick beef sausage
2 teaspoons olive oil
1 small red onion, cut into
    wedges
1/3 cup (90 g) ready-made
    chunky tomato pasta sauce
1 small ripe tomato, peeled,
    seeded and chopped
1 tablespoon chopped fresh
    flat-leaf parsley

1 Bring a large saucepan of salted water to the boil and cook the pasta until *al dente*. Drain, reserving 1/4 cup (60 ml) of the water.
2 Meanwhile, prick the sausage all over with a fork. Heat a non-stick frying pan and cook the sausage over medium heat, turning often, for 5 minutes, or until cooked. Cut into thick diagonal slices and set aside.
3 Clean the frying pan and heat the oil. Cook the onion wedges over medium heat for 3 minutes, or until soft. Add the tomato pasta sauce and the tomato. Cook for 3–4 minutes, or until the tomato has softened. Add the sliced sausage and heat through for 1 minute.
4 Toss the pasta through the sauce, adding a little of the reserved pasta water, if necessary. Sprinkle with parsley and serve.

NUTRITION PER SERVE
Protein 12 g; Fat 18 g; Carbohydrate 44 g; Dietary Fibre 7.5 g; Cholesterol 17 mg; 1605 kJ (383 cal)

Cut the cooked sausage into thick slices on the diagonal.

Add the pasta sauce and tomato to the pan and cook until the tomato is soft.

Toss the pasta through the sauce to warm through.

SPAGHETTI WITH TUNA, BASIL AND CAPERS

Preparation time: 10 minutes
Total cooking time: 15 minutes
Serves 1

125 g spaghetti
2 teaspoons extra virgin
    olive oil
1 clove garlic, crushed
95 g can tuna in brine, drained
    and broken into chunks

1/2 cup (15 g) fresh basil
    leaves, torn
2 vine-ripened tomatoes,
    roughly chopped
1 tablespoon capers, roughly
    chopped
2 tablespoons freshly grated
    Parmesan

1 Bring a large saucepan of salted water to the boil, add the spaghetti and cook until *al dente*. Drain and return to the pan.
2 Meanwhile, heat the oil in a small saucepan, add the garlic and tuna and cook over medium heat for 1 minute, or until the garlic is fragrant and the tuna is warmed through.
3 Add the tuna mixture, basil, tomato, capers and Parmesan to the spaghetti and mix together well. Season with salt and freshly ground black pepper and serve with crusty bread.

NUTRITION PER SERVE
Protein 48 g; Fat 20 g; Carbohydrate 93 g; Dietary Fibre 9.5 g; Cholesterol 60 mg; 3147 kJ (752 cal)

Using a sharp knife, roughly chop the vine-ripened tomatoes.

Cook the garlic and tuna over medium heat for 1 minute.

Mix together the spaghetti, tuna, basil, tomato, capers and Parmesan.

PRAWNS WITH JASMINE RICE

Preparation time: 15 minutes
Total cooking time: 30 minutes
Serves 1

2 teaspoons peanut oil
2 spring onions, sliced
1½ teaspoons finely chopped
    fresh ginger
1 teaspoon finely sliced lemon
    grass, white part only
½ teaspoon crushed coriander
    seeds (see Note)
½ cup (100 g) jasmine rice
1 cup (250 ml) vegetable
    stock
1 teaspoon shredded lime
    rind
250 g raw prawns, peeled,
    deveined and chopped
2 teaspoons lime juice
3 tablespoons fresh coriander
    leaves
fish sauce, optional

1 Heat the oil in a saucepan, add the spring onion and cook over low heat for 4 minutes, or until soft. Add the ginger, lemon grass, coriander seeds and rice, and stir for 1 minute.
2 Add the stock and lime rind and bring to the boil while stirring. Reduce the heat to very low and cook, covered, for 15–20 minutes, or until the rice is tender.
3 Remove the pan from the heat and stir in the prawns. Cover and leave for 4–5 minutes, or until the prawns are cooked. Add the lime juice and coriander leaves and flake the rice with a fork. Sprinkle with a few drops of fish sauce, if desired. Serve with steamed snow peas and lime wedges.

NUTRITION PER SERVE
Protein 59 g; Fat 12 g; Carbohydrate 80 g; Dietary Fibre 3 g; Cholesterol 373 mg; 2850 kJ (681 cal)

COOK'S FILE

Note: To crush coriander seeds, place in a small plastic bag and, using a rolling pin, crush until fine.

Peel and devein the prawns and cut them into 1 cm pieces.

Add the ginger, lemon grass, coriander seeds and rice to the saucepan.

Add the lime juice and coriander leaves and flake the rice with a fork.

VEGETABLE RISOTTO

Preparation time: 15 minutes
Total cooking time: 30 minutes
Serves 1

1 tablespoon olive oil
1/2 small onion, finely chopped
1 clove garlic, finely chopped
1/2 cup (110 g) arborio rice
2–2 1/2 cups (500–625 ml)
    chicken or vegetable stock
1/2 small zucchini, diced
1/2 small red capsicum, diced
1 cup (35 g) lightly packed,
    shredded English spinach
    leaves
1 tablespoon chopped fresh
    flat-leaf parsley
2 teaspoons grated Parmesan
shaved Parmesan, to garnish

1 Heat the oil in a saucepan and cook the onion and garlic over low heat for 1–2 minutes, or until soft. Add the rice and stir for 1 minute, or until well coated.

2 In a separate saucepan, heat the stock and keep it at simmering point. Add 1/2 cup (125 ml) hot stock to the rice, stirring constantly over medium heat until the liquid is absorbed. Continue adding more stock, 1/2 cup (125 ml) at a time, stirring constantly for 20–25 minutes, or until all the stock is absorbed and the rice is tender and creamy in texture. Once 1 1/2 cups (375 ml) of the stock have been added, stir in the zucchini, capsicum and spinach.

3 Remove from the heat, add the parsley and Parmesan, and stir until the Parmesan has melted. Season with salt and pepper and serve with shaved Parmesan and crusty bread.

NUTRITION PER SERVE
Protein 13 g; Fat 22 g; Carbohydrate 95 g; Dietary Fibre 6.5 g; Cholesterol 5 mg; 2645 kJ (630 cal)

COOK'S FILE

Variation: Add a small, sliced chicken breast fillet with the onion and garlic and continue with the recipe.

Add the rice to the saucepan and stir until well coated.

Ladle hot stock over the rice and stir until absorbed.

Once most of the stock has been added, stir in the zucchini, capsicum and spinach.

CHORIZO PILAF

Preparation time: 15 minutes +
   10 minutes standing
Total cooking time: 25 minutes
Serves 1

2 teaspoons butter
1/2 onion, thinly sliced
1 clove garlic, crushed
1 (100 g) chorizo sausage,
   thinly sliced on the diagonal
1/2 cup (100 g) long-grain rice
1 small bay leaf
1 cup (250 ml) chicken stock
1/4 cup (40 g) frozen peas
30 g sun-dried capsicums in oil,
   drained, thinly sliced
2 spring onions, finely chopped
shaved Parmesan, to garnish

1 Melt the butter in a small saucepan, add the onion and garlic and cook, stirring, over medium heat for 2 minutes, or until the onion starts to soften. Add the sausage and cook, stirring, for 1 minute. Add the rice and bay leaf and stir until the rice is coated in the butter.

2 Add the chicken stock and bring to the boil, cooking until tunnels appear in the rice. Stir quickly, then reduce the heat to low and cook, covered, for 15–20 minutes, or until the rice is just tender. Sprinkle the peas and capsicum strips over the rice. Cover, remove from the heat and leave to stand for a further 10 minutes. Add the spring onion and fluff with a fork. Serve topped with Parmesan.

NUTRITION PER SERVE
Protein 20 g; Fat 32 g; Carbohydrate 11 g; Dietary Fibre 6.5 g; Cholesterol 85 mg; 1705 kJ (405 cal)

Thinly slice the chorizo sausage on the diagonal.

Add the stock and cook until tunnels appear in the rice.

Sprinkle the peas and sun-dried capsicum strips over the rice mixture.

KEDGEREE

Preparation time: 10 minutes
Total cooking time: 25 minutes
Serves 1

1/3 cup (65 g) long-grain rice
150 g smoked cod
1 lemon slice
1 bay leaf
1 egg, hard-boiled
15 g butter
1/2 small onion, finely chopped
1–2 teaspoons mild curry paste

1 teaspoon finely chopped fresh
   parsley
2 tablespoons cream

1 Bring a small saucepan of water to the boil, add the rice and boil rapidly for 10–12 minutes, or until tender.
2 Place the cod in a deep frying pan with the lemon and bay leaf, cover with water and simmer for 6 minutes, or until cooked. Remove with a slotted spoon and break into flakes.
3 Cut the egg in half. Finely chop one half and cut the other half into quarters to garnish.

4 Melt the butter in a small frying pan, add the onion and cook over medium heat for 3 minutes, or until soft. Add the curry paste and cook for another 2 minutes. Add the rice and carefully stir through, cooking for 2–3 minutes, or until heated through. Stir in the parsley, cod, chopped egg and cream. Garnish with the egg quarters and serve with toast.

NUTRITION PER SERVE
Protein 50 g; Fat 38 g; Carbohydrate 152 g; Dietary Fibre 6 g; Cholesterol 373 mg; 4805 kJ (1148 cal)

Simmer the cod in a deep frying pan for 6 minutes, or until cooked.

Add the curry paste to the onion and cook for 2 minutes.

Stir the parsley, fish, chopped egg and cream in with the rice.

EASY EVERYDAY DINNERS

BAKED SNAPPER WITH HERBS

Preparation time: 15 minutes
Total cooking time: 40 minutes
Serves 1

½ lemon, sliced
½ teaspoon finely grated
    lemon rind
3 sprigs fresh mint, leaves
    removed, reserving stalks
3 sprigs fresh basil, leaves
    removed, reserving stalks
1 clove garlic, finely sliced
400 g whole baby snapper,
    scaled and gutted
1 tablespoon white wine
1 tablespoon olive oil

1 Preheat the oven to moderately hot 200°C (400°F/Gas 6). Place two sheets of foil large enough to wrap up the entire fish on a baking tray and top with two pieces of baking paper. Lay the lemon slices in the centre of the baking paper.

2 Place half the lemon rind in a bowl with the mint leaves, basil and garlic, mix well and use to stuff the cavity of the fish. Place the reserved stalks over the lemon slices and lay the fish on top.

3 Sprinkle the remaining rind over the fish and season with salt and freshly ground black pepper. Mix together the wine and oil and pour over the fish. Wrap in the foil and baking paper to fully enclose.

4 Bake for 30–40 minutes, or until cooked. The flesh should be white and flake from the bone easily. Serve with steamed potato wedges and salad.

NUTRITION PER SERVE
Protein 80 g; Fat 26 g; Carbohydrate 0.5 g; Dietary Fibre 0.76 g; Cholesterol 244 mg; 2401 kJ (575 cal)

Stuff the fish with the lemon rind, mint, basil and garlic mixture.

Bake the fish for 30–40 minutes, or until the flesh is white and flakes from the bone.

LEMON LAMB KEBABS

Preparation time: 10 minutes +
  30 minutes marinating
Total cooking time: 12 minutes
Serves 1

2 tablespoons lemon juice
1 tablespoon extra virgin
  olive oil
1 small clove garlic, crushed
1 teaspoon chopped fresh
  rosemary
100 g lamb fillets, cubed
2 spring onions, cut into
  2 cm lengths
6 stuffed green olives
¼ lemon, cut into small wedges

1 Place the lemon juice, olive oil, garlic and rosemary in a bowl and mix well. Add the lamb and toss to coat. Season with freshly ground black pepper. Cover and marinate for 30 minutes, tossing occasionally.
2 Thread the marinated lamb, spring onion, olives and lemon wedges alternately onto skewers and place on a grill tray.
3 Cook under a hot grill, basting with the marinade and turning during cooking, for 5–6 minutes each side, or until the lamb is cooked. Place the kebabs on a bed of steamed rice and serve with plain yoghurt.

NUTRITION PER SERVE
Protein 25 g; Fat 25 g; Carbohydrate 3.5 g; Dietary Fibre 4 g; Cholesterol 66 mg; 1414 kJ (338 cal)

COOK'S FILE

Note: If using wooden skewers, soak them in water for 30 minutes or cover the ends with foil to prevent burning.

Add the lamb fillets to the lemon juice mixture and toss to coat.

Thread the marinated lamb, spring onion, olives and lemon wedges onto the skewers.

Baste the kebabs with the marinade during cooking.

UDON NOODLES WITH BOK CHOY AND SHIITAKE MUSHROOMS

Preparation time: 10 minutes
Total cooking time: 5 minutes
Serves 1

1 head (500 g) baby bok choy
1 tablespoon oil
4 fresh shiitake mushrooms, quartered (see Note)
50 g bean sprouts
200 g packet fresh Udon noodles, blanched in boiling water and drained well

2 teaspoons kecap manis
1 teaspoon soy sauce
2 teaspoons oyster sauce
1/4 teaspoon sesame oil
1 clove garlic, finely chopped

1 Cut the bok choy head into quarters by slicing lengthways through the stem and leaves.

2 Heat the oil in a frying pan and cook the bok choy and mushrooms over medium heat for 2 minutes, or until the bok choy is slightly wilted. Place in a bowl with the bean sprouts and noodles and toss to combine. Set aside and keep warm.

3 Place the kecap manis, soy sauce, oyster sauce, sesame oil and garlic in a small saucepan and stir over low heat for 1–2 minutes, or until heated through. Pour the sauce over the vegetables and noodles, toss well and serve immediately.

NUTRITION PER SERVE
Protein 30 g; Fat 23 g; Carbohydrate 47 g; Dietary Fibre 25 g; Cholesterol 0 mg; 2169 kJ (518 cal)

COOK'S FILE

Note: When buying fresh shiitake mushrooms, try to select firm, dry mushrooms with a pungent smell.

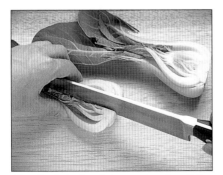

Cut the bok choy into quarters by slicing through the stem and leaves.

Cook the bok choy and mushrooms until the bok choy is slightly wilted.

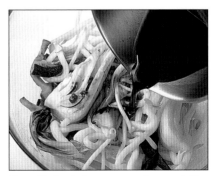

Pour the heated sauce over the vegetables and noodles and toss well.

SPICED CHICKEN WITH PEAR

Preparation time: 10 minutes
Total cooking time: 20 minutes
Serves 1

1 chicken breast fillet
1 tablespoon seasoned plain
   flour
2 teaspoons olive oil
10 g butter
1 small onion, finely sliced
1/2 teaspoon ground ginger
1/2 teaspoon ground cinnamon
1/2 cup (125 ml) apple juice
1/2 small chicken stock cube

1 teaspoon honey
1 small pear, peeled, cored and
   quartered (see Note)

1 Coat the chicken with the flour and shake off any excess. Heat the oil in a frying pan and cook the chicken over medium heat for 2–3 minutes each side, or until lightly browned. Remove and keep warm. Melt the butter in the pan, add the onion and spices and cook for 2–3 minutes, or until golden. Stir in the apple juice, stock cube and honey, bring to the boil, then reduce the heat and simmer for 2 minutes.
2 Return the chicken to the frying pan, add the pear quarters and simmer, covered, for 5 minutes. Turn

the chicken and pear over and simmer for a further 5 minutes, or until the chicken is cooked through.
3 Place the chicken and pear on a warm plate, spoon on the sauce and serve with steamed couscous.

NUTRITION PER SERVE
Protein 30 g; Fat 20 g; Carbohydrate 45 g; Dietary Fibre 4.5 g; Cholesterol 85 mg; 2067 kJ (494 cal)

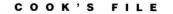

COOK'S FILE

Note: Beurre bosc (brown) pears are ideal for this recipe. Choose a pear with a dark, cinnamon-brown skin. The flesh should be aromatic, white and juicy.

Cook the chicken fillet for 2–3 minutes on each side, or until lightly browned.

Add the apple juice, stock cube and honey and bring to the boil.

Turn the chicken and pear over and simmer for a further 5 minutes.

Process the beans and garlic in a food processor or blender.

Cook the lamb cutlets for 2–3 minutes each side, or until cooked.

LAMB CUTLETS WITH RED WINE SAUCE AND BEAN PUREE

Preparation time: 20 minutes +
    30 minutes marinating
Total cooking time: 15 minutes
Serves 1

1 tablespoon extra virgin
    olive oil
1 clove garlic, thinly sliced
2 sprigs fresh thyme
2–3 lamb cutlets
310 g can cannellini beans
    (see Note)
1 small clove garlic,
    crushed
200 ml beef stock
1 tablespoon olive oil
1/3 cup (80 ml) red wine
1 tablespoon tomato paste
1 tablespoon soft brown
    sugar
fresh sprigs thyme, extra,
    to serve

1 Place the extra virgin olive oil, garlic and thyme in a bowl and mix together well. Add the lamb cutlets and toss well to coat. Season with freshly ground black pepper and marinate for 30 minutes.
2 Rinse and drain half the cannellini beans, place in a food processor or blender with the crushed garlic clove and process until smooth. With the machine running, gradually add 3 teaspoons of the stock and process to form a smooth purée. Season with salt and ground black pepper, place in a small saucepan and gently heat.
3 Heat the olive oil in a small frying pan over medium heat and cook the drained cutlets for 2–3 minutes each side, or until cooked. Remove from the pan and cover to keep warm.
4 In the same pan, add the red wine and stir, scraping the bottom to remove any sediment. Add the remaining stock, tomato paste and sugar to the pan, then reduce the heat and simmer for 5 minutes, or until the sauce has reduced by half.

Add the stock, tomato paste and sugar to the pan and simmer.

5 To serve, place the bean purée on a plate and arrange the lamb cutlets on top. Spoon on the wine sauce, top with the extra thyme sprigs and serve with steamed asparagus and crusty bread.

NUTRITION PER SERVE
Protein 44 g; Fat 48 g; Carbohydrate 37 g; Dietary Fibre 22 g; Cholesterol 72 mg; 3387 kJ (809 cal)

COOK'S FILE

Note: This recipe only uses half a 310 g can of cannellini beans. To keep the remainder, remove from the can and store in an airtight container in the refrigerator for up to a week. Add the leftover beans to vegetable soup.

MOROCCAN BEEF KEBABS WITH FRUIT AND ALMOND COUSCOUS

Preparation time: 10 minutes +
  30 minutes marinating
Total cooking time: 10 minutes
Serves 1

100 g rump steak, cut into
  2 cm cubes
2 teaspoons olive oil
1 clove garlic, finely chopped
1/2 teaspoon ground cumin
1/4 teaspoon ground coriander
1 tablespoon chopped fresh
  coriander leaves
1 teaspoon lemon juice
1/2 onion, cut into wedges

Fruit and almond couscous
1/3 cup (60 g) couscous
1/3 cup (80 ml) boiling beef
  stock
2 tablespoons slivered almonds,
  toasted
2 tablespoons sultanas
1 1/2 teaspoons ground cumin
1 teaspoon ground coriander

1 If using wooden skewers, soak in water for 30 minutes to prevent burning during cooking. Place the beef, olive oil, garlic, spices, coriander leaves, lemon juice and ground black pepper to taste in a bowl, mix together well and marinate for 30 minutes, or overnight if time permits.
2 Thread the beef onto the skewers, alternating with the onion wedges.

Place on a grill tray and cook under a hot grill for 3–4 minutes on each side, or until cooked through, brushing with the marinade during cooking.
3 To make the fruit and almond couscous, place the couscous in a bowl, add the beef stock and leave for 3 minutes, or until all the stock has been absorbed. Fluff up the couscous with a fork and stir in the slivered almonds, sultanas, ground cumin and ground coriander. Season with salt and freshly ground black pepper and serve with the beef kebabs and naan bread.

NUTRITION PER SERVE
Protein 30 g; Fat 29 g; Carbohydrate 63 g; Dietary Fibre 4.5 g; Cholesterol 67 mg; 2092 kJ (500 cal)

Combine the beef, olive oil, garlic, spices, coriander leaves, lemon juice and pepper.

Grill the kebabs until cooked through, brushing with the marinade.

Fluff up the couscous with a fork and add the almonds, sultanas and spices.

COCONUT NOODLES WITH ROAST PUMPKIN, CARROT AND ZUCCHINI

Preparation time: 15 minutes
Total cooking time: 30 minutes
Serves 1

100 g pumpkin, cut into
    2.5 cm chunks
1 small carrot, cut into
    2.5 cm pieces
1 tablespoon oil
1 clove garlic, crushed
1 zucchini, cut into 2.5 cm slices

200 g Udon or egg noodles
1 small onion, chopped
140 ml coconut milk
1/4 cup (7 g) fresh coriander
    leaves
1 small red chilli, finely
    chopped
1 lime, quartered, to serve

1 Preheat the oven to hot 220°C (425°F/Gas 7). Place the pumpkin and carrot in an ovenproof dish. Combine half the oil with the garlic, pour over the vegetables and bake for 15 minutes. Add the zucchini and bake for 15 minutes more.

2 Place the noodles in a bowl, pour in enough boiling water to cover. Stand for 5 minutes, then drain.

3 Meanwhile, heat the remaining oil in a frying pan and cook the onion over medium heat for 3 minutes, or until golden. Add the vegetables, coconut milk and noodles and simmer for 2 minutes. Stir in the coriander leaves and chilli and serve with a squeeze of lime.

NUTRITION PER SERVE
Protein 35 g; Fat 50 g; Carbohydrate 162 g; Dietary Fibre 15 g; Cholesterol 36 mg; 5238 kJ (1250 cal)

Combine half the oil and the garlic and pour over the vegetables.

Cover the noodles with boiling water for 5 minutes, then drain well.

Add the vegetables, coconut milk and noodles and simmer for 2 minutes.

SUNDAY SPATCHCOCK ROAST

Preparation time: 10 minutes
Total cooking time: 45 minutes
Serves 1

1 spatchcock
1/2 small onion, peeled
200 g potato, cut into chunks
1 zucchini, halved lengthways
1 tablespoon olive oil
1/2 tablespoon fresh rosemary
    leaves
1/2 teaspoon plain flour
1/4 cup (60 ml) red wine

1 Preheat the oven to moderately hot 200°C (400°F/Gas 6). Rinse the cavity of the spatchcock and pat dry. Insert the onion into the cavity and tie the legs together with string.
2 Season the skin with salt and freshly ground black pepper and place in a baking dish. Place the cut vegetables around the spatchcock, drizzle with the olive oil and sprinkle with the rosemary.
3 Cook in the oven for 30–40 minutes, or until tender and golden. Remove the spatchcock and vegetables from the dish, cover loosely with foil and set aside in a warm place.
4 Drain off any excess fat from the dish and place on the stove over medium heat. Add the flour and wine and whisk over the heat until the gravy has reduced and thickened.
5 To serve, remove the string from the legs, carve the spatchcock and place it on a warmed serving plate with the vegetables and spoon over the gravy.

NUTRITION PER SERVE
Protein 110 g; Fat 40 g; Carbohydrate 30 g; Dietary Fibre 5.5 g; Cholesterol 345 mg; 4080 kJ (975 cal)

COOK'S FILE

Note: Spatchcock is a great way to prepare roast chicken for one, using baby chickens which are about 6 weeks old and weigh 500 g. The term spatchcock is often used to refer to the baby chicken, but is really related to the preparation of the bird— cooked in a hurry—where the chicken is flattened, seasoned, brushed with oil and grilled for about 15 minutes.

Tie the legs of the spatchcock together with string.

Drizzle olive oil over the bird and vegetables and sprinkle with rosemary.

Cook in the oven for 30–40 minutes, or until tender and golden.

Add the flour and wine to the baking dish and whisk until thickened.

PORK WITH HERBS AND PROSCIUTTO

Preparation time: 15 minutes
Total cooking time: 25 minutes
Serves 1

3 long sprigs fresh oregano
3 paper-thin slices prosciutto,
    folded in half lengthways
1 (200 g) pork fillet,
    trimmed
1 tablespoon oil
1/4 cup (60 ml) white wine

100 ml chicken stock
1 tablespoon Worcestershire
    sauce

1 Preheat the oven to moderate 180°C (350°F/Gas 4). Carefully wrap the oregano and prosciutto alternately around the pork fillet, securing with toothpicks.
2 Heat the oil in a non-stick frying pan, add the pork and cook over medium–high heat, turning to brown on all sides. Transfer to an oven tray and bake for 10–15 minutes, or until cooked through.

3 Add the white wine to the frying pan and bring to the boil, scraping the bottom of the pan to remove any sediment. Add the chicken stock and Worcestershire sauce and boil until the sauce has reduced by half.
4 To serve, remove the toothpicks, slice the fillet and place on a serving plate, then pour on the sauce. Accompany with mashed potato and steamed green vegetables.

NUTRITION PER SERVE
Protein 50 g; Fat 25 g; Carbohydrate 5 g; Dietary Fibre 0 g; Cholesterol 106 mg; 1935 kJ (460 cal)

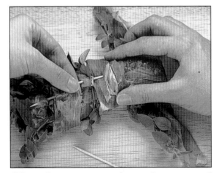

Wrap the oregano and prosciutto around the pork and secure with toothpicks.

Bake in the oven for 10–15 minutes, or until cooked through.

Add the chicken stock and Worcestershire sauce to the pan and bring to the boil.

FISH CUTLET WITH ORANGE, MUSTARD AND DILL SAUCE AND CRUNCHY WEDGES

Preparation time: 15 minutes
Total cooking time: 45 minutes
Serves 1

1 medium potato
cooking oil spray
2 teaspoons olive oil
200 g blue eye or snapper cutlet

¹/₃ cup (80 ml) orange juice
2 teaspoons wholegrain mustard
2 teaspoons chopped fresh dill
1 teaspoon lemon juice

1 Preheat the oven to moderately hot 200°C (400°F/Gas 6). Cut the potato in half and cut each half into three wedges. Place in a small baking dish, spray with cooking oil and season with salt. Bake for 45 minutes, or until golden and crunchy.
2 Meanwhile, heat the oil in a small frying pan and cook the fish cutlet over medium heat for 3 minutes on each side, or until cooked through and golden. Set aside and keep warm.
3 Place the orange juice, mustard, dill and lemon juice in a small saucepan, bring to the boil, then reduce the heat and simmer for 1 minute, or until the mixture has slightly thickened. Spoon the sauce over the fish and serve with the crunchy wedges.

NUTRITION PER SERVE
Protein 46 g; Fat 16 g; Carbohydrate 35 g; Dietary Fibre 3 g; Cholesterol 122 mg; 2232 kJ (533 cal)

Cut the potato in half and then cut each half into three wedges.

Cook the cutlet for 3 minutes on each side, or until cooked through and golden.

Bring the sauce to the boil, then reduce the heat and simmer until it thickens.

CHICKPEA PATTIES WITH CUCUMBER AND TOMATO SALAD

Preparation time: 20 minutes
Total cooking time: 15 minutes
Serves 1

2 teaspoons olive oil
1 small onion, finely chopped
1 clove garlic, finely chopped
1 teaspoon ground cumin
1/2 teaspoon ground coriander
pinch cayenne pepper
300 g can chickpeas,
    drained
2 tablespoons chopped
    fresh parsley
2 teaspoons lemon juice
1 tablespoon plain flour
1/4 teaspoon baking powder
1 egg white
olive oil, extra, for frying

Cucumber and tomato salad
1 small tomato, diced
1 small Lebanese cucumber,
    diced
1 spring onion, finely sliced
2 teaspoons finely chopped
    fresh flat-leaf parsley
2 teaspoons lemon juice

1 Heat the oil in a small non-stick frying pan, add the onion and cook over medium heat for 5 minutes, or until soft. Add the garlic and spices and cook for a further 2 minutes, or until fragrant.
2 Put the onion mixture, chickpeas, parsley, lemon juice, flour, baking powder and egg white in a food processor or blender and process until smooth. Season with salt and freshly ground black pepper. Form into three patties with flour-dusted hands and refrigerate until ready to use.
3 To prepare the salad, combine the tomato, cucumber, onion, parsley and lemon juice. Season with salt and freshly ground black pepper.
4 Heat the extra oil in a large frying pan, add the patties and cook for 2–3 minutes each side, or until golden. Serve with the salad.

NUTRITION PER SERVE
Protein 27 g; Fat 54 g; Carbohydrate 57 g; Dietary Fibre 20 g; Cholesterol 0 mg; 3459 kJ (826 cal)

Form the chickpea mixture into three patties with flour-dusted hands.

Mix together the tomato, cucumber, onion, parsley and lemon juice.

Fry the patties for 2–3 minutes each side, or until golden.

BEEF STROGANOFF

Preparation time: 10 minutes
Total cooking time: 10 minutes
Serves 1

2 teaspoons olive oil
10 g butter
1/2 small onion, sliced
75 g button mushrooms, sliced
1 clove garlic, crushed

150 g rump steak, finely sliced
   across the grain into strips
1/2 cup (125 g) light sour cream
1 tablespoon tomato paste

1 Heat half the oil and butter in a small frying pan and cook the onion over medium heat for 2 minutes, or until soft. Add the mushrooms and garlic and cook for 3 minutes. Remove from the pan and keep warm.
2 Heat the remaining oil and butter in the same frying pan and cook the beef in batches over high heat until browned and tender. Return the mushrooms and onion to the pan and stir through.
3 Remove from the heat and stir in the sour cream and tomato paste. Season and serve immediately with steamed rice and crusty bread.

NUTRITION PER SERVE
Protein 45 g; Fat 47 g; Carbohydrate 11 g; Dietary Fibre 3.5 g; Cholesterol 205 mg; 2659 kJ (635 cal)

Add the mushrooms and garlic to the frying pan and cook for 3 minutes.

Cook the beef in batches until browned and tender.

Remove from the heat and stir in the light sour cream and tomato paste.

54

Cook the apple in the frying pan with the leek until both are golden brown.

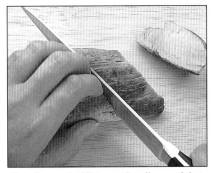

Cut the pork fillet on the diagonal into thick slices.

Add the mustard and cream mixture to the pan and cook until slightly thickened.

Add the butter and milk to the sweet potato and mash with a fork.

PORK WITH APPLE AND SWEET POTATO MASH

Preparation time: 10 minutes
Total cooking time: 25 minutes
Serves 1

1/2 green apple, unpeeled
30 g butter
1 leek, thinly sliced lengthways
1/2 teaspoon soft brown sugar
2 teaspoons oil
1 (200 g) pork fillet, trimmed
100 g orange sweet potato, cubed
1 teaspoon plain flour
2 teaspoons Dijon mustard
100 ml cream
2 teaspoons snipped fresh chives
1–2 teaspoons milk

1 Core the apple and cut it into 6–8 slices. Melt half the butter in a frying pan and add the leek and sugar. Cook for 2–3 minutes, then add the apple and cook for 5 minutes, or until the leek and apple are golden brown. Set aside and keep warm.

2 Heat the oil in the same pan and cook the pork over medium heat for 3–4 minutes each side, or until cooked through. Remove from the pan, cover with foil for 5 minutes and then cut on the diagonal into thick slices.

3 Place the orange sweet potato in a saucepan of water, bring to the boil, then reduce the heat and simmer for 5 minutes, or until tender.

4 Combine the flour and mustard in a small bowl, then add the cream. Add to the frying pan and cook, stirring, until bubbling and slightly thickened. Add the pork and chives and stir until warmed through. Season.

5 Drain the sweet potato when just tender. Add the remaining butter and enough milk to moisten, season and mash with a fork or masher. To serve, arrange the pork over the leek and apple and spoon on the sauce. Serve with the sweet potato mash and steamed vegetables of your choice.

NUTRITION PER SERVE
Protein 52 g; Fat 56 g; Carbohydrate 34 g; Dietary Fibre 6.5 g; Cholesterol 235 mg; 3512 kJ (840 cal)

VEAL MUSHROOM SCALOPPINE

Preparation time: 10 minutes
Total cooking time: 15 minutes
Serves 1

30 g butter
110 g veal escalope (steak)
1 spring onion, finely chopped
90 g button mushrooms, sliced
1 tablespoon dry sherry
2 teaspoons plain flour
1/3 cup (80 ml) boiling beef stock
1 tablespoon cream

1 Melt a third of the butter in a non-stick frying pan over medium heat and cook the veal for 2 minutes each side. Remove from the pan.
2 Melt the remaining butter in the pan, add the spring onion and cook for 1 minute, or until soft. Add the mushrooms and cook for a further 5 minutes. Add the sherry and cook for 1 minute, then sprinkle on the flour and stir for a further 1 minute.
3 Increase the heat to high, add the beef stock and bring to the boil. Return the veal escalope to the pan, then reduce the heat and simmer over low heat for 1 minute. Stir in the cream and heat through. Serve with steamed greens, potatoes and focaccia.

NUTRITION PER SERVE
Protein 30 g; Fat 36 g; Carbohydrate 9 g; Dietary Fibre 3 g; Cholesterol 195 mg; 2063 kJ (493 cal)

Melt the butter in a frying pan and cook the veal for 2 minutes each side.

Sprinkle the flour over the mushroom mixture and stir for 1 minute.

Return the veal to the pan, stir in the cream and heat through.

CHICKEN WITH TOMATO SALSA

Preparation time: 15 minutes
Total cooking time: 10 minutes
Serves 1

¼ cup (35 g) fine polenta
1 tablespoon grated Parmesan
1 egg
1 large chicken breast fillet
1 tablespoon olive oil

Tomato salsa
2 teaspoons lemon juice
1 small clove garlic,
    crushed
½ small firm ripe avocado,
    diced
1 Roma tomato, seeded and
    diced
3 button mushrooms, finely
    sliced
2 teaspoons chopped fresh
    flat-leaf parsley
¼ cup (60 g) ready-made
    tomato salsa

1 Combine the polenta and Parmesan on a large plate. Beat the egg lightly in a shallow dish, add the chicken and coat all over. Drain away the excess egg, then coat the chicken thickly with the polenta mixture, shaking off the excess crumbs.

2 Heat the oil in a heavy-based frying pan and cook the chicken over medium heat for 5 minutes each side, or until golden brown, reducing the heat if it starts to burn. Drain on crumpled paper towels.

3 To make the salsa, whisk the lemon juice and garlic in a bowl. Add the avocado, tomato, mushrooms, parsley and salsa, and season to taste with salt and freshly ground black pepper. Serve the chicken with the salsa and steamed green beans.

NUTRITION PER SERVE
Protein 45 g; Fat 61 g; Carbohydrate 33 g; Dietary Fibre 6 g; Cholesterol 250 mg; 3494 kJ (832 cal)

Dip the chicken in the egg and then coat thickly with the polenta mixture.

Cook the chicken for 5 minutes each side, or until golden brown.

Place the salsa ingredients in a bowl and mix well.

VEAL PARMAGIANA

Preparation time: 15 minutes +
 15 minutes refrigeration
Total cooking time: 15 minutes
Serves 1

2 small thin veal escalopes
 (steaks)
plain flour, for coating
1 egg, lightly beaten
1/2 cup (50 g) dry breadcrumbs
oil, for shallow-frying
1/3 cup (90 g) ready-made
 chunky tomato pasta sauce
1/4 cup (30 g) grated Cheddar
1 tablespoon freshly grated
 Parmesan
1 tablespoon chopped fresh
 flat-leaf parsley
2 teaspoons chopped capers
1 teaspoon grated lemon rind

1 Preheat the oven to moderate 180°C (350°F/Gas 4). Pat the veal dry with paper towels, coat in the flour and shake off any excess. Dip in the egg and then the breadcrumbs. Cover and refrigerate for 15 minutes to firm.
2 Heat the oil to 1 cm in a frying pan. Cook the veal for 2 minutes each side, or until cooked and golden. Drain on paper towels. Place in an ovenproof dish in a single layer. Spoon on the pasta sauce and sprinkle with the cheeses. Bake for 10 minutes, or until hot and the cheeses have melted.
3 Combine the parsley, capers and lemon rind in a small bowl. Spoon over the veal and serve at once.

NUTRITION PER SERVE
Protein 73 g; Fat 43 g; Carbohydrate 60 g; Dietary Fibre 5 g; Cholesterol 384 mg; 3832 kJ (915 cal)

COOK'S FILE

Variation: Try replacing the Cheddar with mozzarella cheese for a more subtle flavour.
If preferred, instead of baking in an oven, you can place the cooked veal steaks on a grill tray and cook under a medium grill for 5 minutes, or until the cheese has melted. Transfer the veal to a serving plate and sprinkle with the parsley, caper and lemon rind mixture.

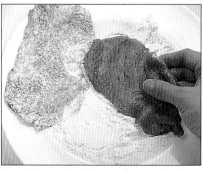

Coat the veal steaks in flour and shake off any excess.

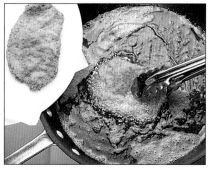

Cook the veal for 2 minutes each side, or until cooked and golden.

Bake for 10 minutes, or until hot and the cheeses have melted.

Combine the parsley, capers and lemon rind in a small bowl.

STEAK WITH MUSTARD SAUCE

Preparation time: 5 minutes
Total cooking time: 12 minutes
Serves 1

30 g butter
1 clove garlic, crushed
¹/₂ cup (25 g) English spinach leaves, torn
125 g fillet steak
¹/₄ cup (60 ml) white wine
2 teaspoons wholegrain mustard
¹/₄ cup (60 ml) cream

1 Heat half the butter in a frying pan, add the garlic and spinach, and cook over medium heat for 2 minutes, or until the spinach is just wilted. Remove from the pan and keep warm. Heat the remaining butter in the pan, add the steak and cook over medium heat for 3–4 minutes each side, or until cooked to your liking. Remove and cover with foil to keep warm.
2 Add the wine, mustard and cream to the pan, scraping the bottom of the pan to remove any sediment. Bring to the boil, then reduce the heat and simmer for 1 minute. Season to taste.
3 Cut the steak across the grain into 5 mm slices. Place the spinach on a serving plate and arrange the steak over it. Spoon on the sauce and serve immediately with potato mash.

NUTRITION PER SERVE
Protein 33 g; Fat 56 g; Carbohydrate 3 g; Dietary Fibre 4.5 g; Cholesterol 242 mg; 2782 kJ (665 cal)

Cook the spinach and garlic for 2 minutes, or until the spinach is just wilted.

Add the wine, mustard and cream, boil then reduce the heat and simmer.

Using a sharp knife, cut the steak across the grain into 5 mm slices.

TUNA IN RICH KAFFIR LIME SAUCE

Preparation time: 5 minutes
Total cooking time: 15 minutes
Serves 1

100 ml cream
100 ml fish stock
4 kaffir lime leaves, finely sliced
1 teaspoon peanut oil
200 g tuna steak, cut into
    3 cm cubes

1 head (500 g) baby bok choy,
    halved and washed

1 Place the cream, fish stock and lime leaves in a small saucepan over low heat. Boil for 15 minutes, stirring occasionally, or until the sauce has reduced and thickened. Keep warm.
2 Meanwhile, heat a wok until very hot, add the oil and swirl to coat the sides. Add the tuna and stir-fry for 2 minutes, or until seared on all sides, but not cooked through. Remove the tuna and keep warm.

3 Add the bok choy to the wok and stir-fry over high heat for 1–2 minutes, or until the leaves are just starting to wilt. Add 1–2 teaspoons water to the bok choy, if necessary, to assist wilting.
4 Place the bok choy and tuna on a serving plate and pour on the sauce. Serve with steamed rice and lime wedges.

NUTRITION PER SERVE
Protein 68 g; Fat 55 g; Carbohydrate 6 g; Dietary Fibre 20 g; Cholesterol 276 mg; 3300 kJ (788 cal)

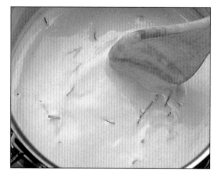

Place the cream, fish stock and lime leaves in a saucepan and simmer.

Quickly stir-fry the tuna until just seared on all sides.

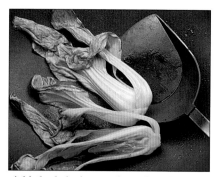

Add the bok choy to the wok and stir-fry until just starting to wilt.

SATAY LAMB

Preparation time: 10 minutes
Total cooking time: 20 minutes
Serves 1

**200 g lamb backstrap or
    loin fillet
2 teaspoons oil
1/2 onion, cut into thin wedges
1 clove garlic, crushed
1 teaspoon red curry paste
1/4 cup (60 g) crunchy peanut
    butter
1/4 cup (60 ml) coconut milk
1 teaspoon kecap manis
2 teaspoons tomato sauce
fresh coriander, to garnish**

1 Trim the lamb of any excess fat and sinew and cut into 2 cm cubes.
2 Heat the oil in a saucepan, add the onion and garlic and cook, stirring, over low heat for 4 minutes, or until the onion is soft. Add the curry paste and cook for 1 minute, then remove from the heat.
3 Add the peanut butter to the pan, return to the heat and stir in the coconut milk and 1/4 cup (60 ml) water. Bring to the boil, stirring so the mixture does not stick. Add the kecap manis and tomato sauce, reduce the heat and simmer for 1 minute, or until thickened slightly.
4 Thread the meat onto 3 skewers, place on a lightly oiled grill tray and brush with the peanut mixture. Cook under a hot grill for 5 minutes each side, or until tender, brushing with the peanut mixture during cooking.
5 Meanwhile, place the remaining peanut mixture in a small saucepan and stir over medium heat for 3–5 minutes, or until heated through. Serve the skewers, garnished with coriander, on a bed of rice with the sauce on the side.

NUTRITION PER SERVE
Protein 60 g; Fat 60 g; Carbohydrate 11 g; Dietary Fibre 8.5 g; Cholesterol 132 mg; 3509 kJ (838 cal)

COOK'S FILE

Note: If using wooden skewers, soak them for 30 minutes prior to grilling to prevent them from burning.

Trim the lamb of any excess fat and sinew and cut into 2 cm cubes.

Simmer the peanut mixture for 1 minute, or until thickened slightly.

Cook the skewers under a hot grill, brushing with the peanut mixture.

Fabulous fast sauces

These quick-as-a-flash sauces can jazz up your favourite dish and transform an easy-to-prepare dinner into a gourmet feast. Try one of these delicious sauces on steak, veal, chicken or seafood.

MUSHROOM SAUCE

Melt 20 g butter in a small saucepan, add 200 g quartered mushrooms and cook over medium heat, stirring, for 2 minutes, or until lightly browned. Add 1/4 cup (60 ml) red wine, 1/3 cup (80 ml) beef stock and 2 tablespoons water, and cook for 6 minutes, or until reduced slightly. Add 1 tablespoon cream and cook for 1 minute. Serve with veal and steamed potatoes with butter and chives.

CORIANDER MAYONNAISE

Place 3/4 cup (25 g) fresh coriander leaves, 2 tablespoons whole-egg mayonnaise, 1 teaspoon French mustard, 2 tablespoons olive oil and 1 teaspoon lime juice in a food processor or blender and process until smooth. Season to taste with salt and freshly ground black pepper. Serve on the side with char-grilled prawns, French fries and lime wedges.

MUSTARD SAUCE

Place 1/4 cup (60 ml) beef stock, 1 finely chopped spring onion, 1 teaspoon red wine vinegar and 2 teaspoons wholegrain mustard in a small saucepan and mix together well. Bring the mixture to the boil and boil for 2 minutes, or until reduced by half. Stir in 1/4 cup (60 g) sour cream and gently heat through without boiling. Serve with filet mignon and lightly steamed asparagus.

BEARNAISE SAUCE

Place 1 tablespoon grated white onion, 2 tablespoons white wine vinegar, 1 tablespoon fresh tarragon leaves, 1/2 teaspoon dried tarragon leaves and 1 tablespoon water in a small saucepan. Bring to the boil, then reduce the heat and simmer for 2–3 minutes, or until the sauce reduces to 2 teaspoons. Remove from the heat. Whisk 2 egg yolks with 1 teaspoon water and add to the pan, combining well. Gradually whisk in 80 g melted butter. Strain the sauce through a fine strainer, season with salt and ground black pepper and stir in 5 shredded fresh tarragon leaves. Serve with char-grilled rib eye steak and char-grilled vegetables.

GREEN PEPPERCORN SAUCE

Melt 5 g butter in a small saucepan, add 1 teaspoon finely chopped onion and cook over low heat for 3–4 minutes, or until soft. Stir in 2 teaspoons roughly chopped green peppercorns in brine. Add 1 tablespoon white wine and cook until evaporated. Add 1/4 cup (60 ml) chicken stock, 1 tablespoon cream and 1 tablespoon sour cream and simmer over low heat until the sauce reaches the desired consistency. Serve with New York steak and steamed bok choy.

MINT JUS

Melt 5 g butter in a small saucepan. Add 1 tablespoon finely chopped onion and cook over medium heat for 2 minutes, or until soft. Add 1 tablespoon white wine, bring to the boil and cook for 1 minute. Add 1/4 cup (60 ml) chicken stock, 1 teaspoon Worcestershire sauce, 1 teaspoon teriyaki sauce and 1/2 cup (10 g) fresh mint leaves. Bring to the boil and cook for 1–2 minutes. Remove from the heat, strain and add 5 shredded fresh mint leaves. Serve with lamb cutlets and roast potatoes.

Clockwise from top left: Mushroom sauce; Coriander mayonnaise; Mustard sauce; Mint jus; Green peppercorn sauce; Bearnaise sauce.

ROASTED SESAME SEED MAYONNAISE

Separate 1 egg and place the yolk in a food processor with 1/2 teaspoon Dijon mustard and 2 teaspoons lemon juice. Process for 30 seconds, or until the mixture is light and creamy. Add 1/4 cup (60 ml) olive oil, mixed with 1 teaspoon sesame oil, to the mixture in a thin stream while the motor is running and process until thickened and combined. Transfer to a bowl and stir through 1 tablespoon toasted sesame seeds and 1/2 teaspoon honey. Season to taste with salt and freshly ground black pepper. Serve with char-grilled tuna steaks and rocket leaves.

MUSTARD AND GHERKIN SAUCE

Melt 5 g butter in a small saucepan. Add 1 teaspoon finely grated onion and cook, stirring, over medium heat for 2 minutes, or until soft. Add 2 teaspoons white wine and cook until nearly evaporated. Add 1/3 cup (80 ml) chicken stock, 1 tablespoon Dijon mustard, 1 teaspoon French mustard and 1 tablespoon water and bring to the boil. Reduce the heat and simmer for 3 minutes, or until reduced by half. Add 1 finely diced gherkin and cook until thickened. Remove from the heat and stir in 2 teaspoons finely chopped fresh flat-leaf parsley. Serve with chicken skewers and a green salad.

ONION GRAVY

Melt 15 g butter in a small saucepan over medium heat. Add 1/2 thinly sliced small onion and cook, stirring, for 2–3 minutes, or until softened. Stir in 2 teaspoons plain flour and cook for 30 seconds, or until pale and foaming. Remove from the heat and gradually stir in 1/3 cup (80 ml) beef stock. Return to the heat and stir constantly until the sauce boils and thickens. Reduce the heat and simmer for 1 minute. Season. Serve with beef patties or rissoles and crispy potato wedges seasoned with salt. Or you can serve the rissole on a hamburger bun and top with the onion gravy and some lettuce leaves.

LEMON HOLLANDAISE SAUCE

Place 1/4 cup (60 ml) dry white wine in a small saucepan, bring to the boil and boil until it has reduced to 1 1/2 tablespoons. Place 2 egg yolks in a small heatproof bowl, stir in the wine and season. Place the bowl over a pan of simmering water and whisk until it thickens. Gradually add 75 g melted butter, whisking continuously. If the mixture thickens too much, add 1 teaspoon water to prevent it curdling. Remove from the heat and stir in 1 tablespoon lemon juice. Serve with grilled salmon fillets, seasoned with freshly ground black pepper, and steamed asparagus.

PESTO BUTTER

Blanch 1/2 cup (25 g) fresh basil leaves in salted boiling water for 20 seconds, drain and finely chop. Combine the chopped basil leaves, 1 crushed garlic clove, 1 teaspoon grated Parmesan and 30 g softened butter in a bowl and season. Spread the mixture on a sheet of baking paper in an even layer about 5 mm thick, and place in the refrigerator to harden. Cut into small cubes and place over roast chicken thigh cutlets. Melt the butter for a few seconds before serving with roast potatoes and green beans.

TARRAGON SAUCE

Melt 5 g butter in a small saucepan, add 1 teaspoon finely chopped onion and cook, stirring, over low heat for 3–4 minutes, or until the onion is soft. Add 1 tablespoon white wine and 2 tablespoons fresh tarragon leaves and cook, stirring, for 1 minute. Add 1/2 cup (125 ml) chicken stock and 1 tablespoon cream. Reduce the heat and simmer for 5 minutes, or until the sauce reaches the desired consistency. Strain and add 3 finely shredded fresh tarragon leaves. Serve with chicken and steamed sugar snap peas.

Clockwise from top left: *Roasted sesame seed mayonnaise; Mustard and gherkin sauce; Onion gravy; Tarragon sauce; Pesto butter; Lemon hollandaise sauce.*

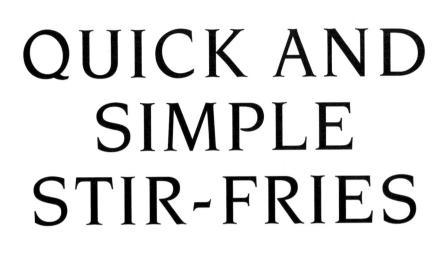

QUICK AND SIMPLE STIR-FRIES

LIME AND GARLIC PRAWNS WITH SUGAR SNAP PEAS

Preparation time: 10 minutes
Total cooking time: 3 minutes
Serves 1

2 tablespoons lime juice
1 tablespoon soy sauce
2 teaspoons honey
1 teaspoon peanut oil
1 clove garlic, crushed
2 kaffir lime leaves,
    shredded
4 baby corn, halved
    lengthways
50 g sugar snap peas
8 raw medium prawns,
    peeled and deveined,
    tails intact
3 tablespoons fresh coriander
    leaves, chopped

1 Place the lime juice, soy sauce and honey in a small bowl and stir until the honey dissolves.
2 Heat a wok over high heat, add the oil and swirl to coat the sides. Add the garlic, lime leaves and baby corn and stir-fry for 1–2 minutes.
3 Add the sugar snap peas, prawns and lime juice mixture and stir-fry for a further minute, or until the prawns are cooked through. Stir in the coriander leaves and serve immediately with steamed rice.

NUTRITION PER SERVE
Protein 27 g; Fat 5.5 g; Carbohydrate 23 g; Dietary Fibre 5 g; Cholesterol 150 mg; 930 kJ (222 cal)

COOK'S FILE

Note: To keep kaffir lime leaves fresh, keep them in an airtight container or plastic bag in the freezer. They will defrost within 1 minute.

Stir the lime juice, soy sauce and honey until the honey dissolves.

Add the sugar snap peas, prawns and lime juice mixture to the wok and stir-fry.

STIR-FRIED CHICKEN WITH SNOW PEAS

Preparation time: 10 minutes
Total cooking time: 10 minutes
Serves 1

2 teaspoons oil
1/2 teaspoon sesame oil
200 g chicken breast fillet,
    cut into strips
1/2 leek, white part only,
    julienned
1 clove garlic, crushed
50 g snow peas, sliced in half
    on the diagonal
1 tablespoon soy sauce
2 teaspoons mirin
1/2 teaspoon soft brown sugar
fresh coriander leaves,
    to garnish

1 Heat a wok over high heat, add the oils and swirl to coat the sides. Add the sliced chicken breast and stir-fry for 3–4 minutes, or until just cooked.
2 Add the leek and garlic and stir-fry for 1–2 minutes, or until the leek is soft and golden. Add the snow peas and stir-fry for 1 minute. Add the soy sauce, mirin and sugar to the wok, and toss well. Season with salt and freshly ground black pepper. Garnish with the coriander leaves and serve immediately with steamed rice.

NUTRITION PER SERVE
Protein 50 g; Fat 17 g; Carbohydrate 10 g; Dietary Fibre 4 g; Cholesterol 100 mg; 1664 kJ (398 cal)

Stir-fry the chicken in the combined oils until just cooked.

Add the soy sauce, mirin and sugar to the wok and toss well.

STIR-FRIED PORK AND GREEN BEANS WITH GINGER SAUCE

Preparation time: 15 minutes
Total cooking time: 10 minutes
Serves 1

1/4 cup (60 ml) soy sauce
1 1/2 tablespoons white or
    rice wine vinegar
1/2 teaspoon sugar
pinch dried chilli flakes
1 teaspoon cornflour
1 (200) g pork fillet, trimmed
    and cut into thin slices
1 tablespoon peanut oil

100 g green beans, cut into
    4 cm lengths
1 clove garlic, chopped
3 teaspoons coarsely grated
    fresh ginger

1 Place the soy sauce, vinegar, sugar, chilli flakes, cornflour and 1/3 cup (80 ml) water in a bowl and mix well. Add the pork and toss to coat.
2 Heat a wok or large frying pan over high heat, add half the oil and swirl to coat the sides. Drain the pork, reserving the liquid, and add to the wok. Stir-fry over high heat for 1–2 minutes, or until browned. Remove the pork from the wok.
3 Heat the remaining oil, add the beans and stir-fry for 3–4 minutes. Add the garlic and ginger and stir-fry for 1 minute, or until fragrant. Return the pork and any juices to the pan and add the reserved marinade. Bring to the boil and cook, stirring, for 1–2 minutes, or until slightly thickened. Serve with steamed rice.

NUTRITION PER SERVE
Protein 51 g; Fat 23 g; Carbohydrate 11 g; Dietary Fibre 3.5 g; Cholesterol 100 mg; 1917 kJ (458 cal)

COOK'S FILE

Note: Rice wine vinegar is made by oxidising beer or wine made from fermented rice starch.

Add the pork to the wok and stir-fry until browned.

Heat the remaining oil and stir-fry the green beans.

Return the pork and reserved marinade to the wok and toss well.

STIR-FRIED BLACK BEAN AND CHILLI MUSSELS

Preparation time: 10 minutes
Total cooking time: 8 minutes
Serves 1

2 teaspoons salted black beans, rinsed well
1 teaspoon finely chopped fresh ginger
1 clove garlic, chopped
3 teaspoons sugar
2 teaspoons oyster sauce
1 teaspoon soy sauce
2 teaspoons oil
1 small red chilli, seeded and thinly sliced
300 g black mussels, scrubbed and debearded (see Note)
1 teaspoon cornflour
2 spring onions, sliced on the diagonal
fresh coriander leaves, to serve

1 Place the black beans, ginger, garlic, sugar, oyster sauce and soy sauce in a small bowl and mash with a fork until just combined.

2 Heat a wok over high heat, add the oil and swirl to coat the sides. Add the chilli and stir-fry for 30 seconds, then add the black bean mixture and stir-fry for 1 minute, or until fragrant. Add the mussels and stir-fry for 3–5 minutes, or until they open. Discard any that do not open. Reduce the heat to low.

3 Place the cornflour and 1/4 cup (60 ml) water in a bowl and stir until smooth. Add to the wok and bring to the boil, stirring until the sauce boils and thickens. Stir through the spring onion and sprinkle with the coriander leaves. Serve with jasmine rice.

NUTRITION PER SERVE
Protein 38 g; Fat 7.5 g; Carbohydrate 19 g; Dietary Fibre 1.5 g; Cholesterol 243 mg; 1240 kJ (295 cal)

COOK'S FILE

Note: When buying mussels make sure they are fresh and alive. Live mussels will have tightly closed shells with some that may be slightly opened. Give the shells a tap and if they close this will indicate that they are still alive. Discard any with broken or cracked shells. Always buy extra to allow for the ones that are cracked or do not open during cooking.

Mix together the black beans, ginger, garlic, sugar, oyster and soy sauce.

Stir-fry the mussels for 3–5 minutes, or until they open.

Add the cornflour mixture to the wok and bring to the boil.

Mix together the olive oil, lemon rind, lemon juice, spring onion and oregano.

Cut the squid hoods in half and then slice into thin strips lengthways.

Add the squid strips to the salt and pepper mixture and toss to coat.

SALT AND PEPPER SQUID WITH OLIVE OIL AND OREGANO

Preparation time: 10 minutes
Total cooking time: 5 minutes
Serves 1

2 tablespoons olive oil
1/2 teaspoon grated lemon rind
1 tablespoon lemon juice
1 spring onion, finely sliced
1 teaspoon chopped fresh
    oregano
250 g squid hoods
1 teaspoon sea salt
1 teaspoon ground black pepper

1 teaspoon olive oil, extra
20 g mixed salad leaves

1 To make the dressing, mix together the olive oil, lemon rind, lemon juice, spring onion and oregano.
2 Pat the squid hoods dry with paper towels and cut them in half and then into thin strips lengthways.
3 Place the salt and pepper in a bowl, mix well and add the squid strips. Toss to evenly coat.
4 Heat a wok over high heat, add the extra oil and swirl to coat the sides. Cook the squid strips, in two batches, stir-frying for 1–2 minutes, or until tender. Serve on the salad leaves and drizzle with the dressing.

Cook the squid strips in two batches over high heat.

NUTRITION PER SERVE
Protein 40 g; Fat 45 g; Carbohydrate 1 g; Dietary Fibre 1 g; Cholesterol 498 mg; 2449 kJ (585 cal)

THAI-STYLE CHICKEN AND BASIL STIR-FRY

Preparation time: 15 minutes
Total cooking time: 7 minutes
Serves 1

1 tablespoon fish sauce
1 tablespoon lime juice
1/2 small tomato, diced
1/3 cup (10 g) loosely packed
    fresh Thai basil leaves
3 teaspoons peanut or
    vegetable oil
2 cloves garlic, thinly sliced
2 spring onions, finely sliced
1/2 small red chilli, seeded,
    thinly sliced
1 chicken breast fillet, thinly
    sliced
70 g snow peas, topped and
    tailed

1 Place the fish sauce, lime juice, tomato, basil and 1 tablespoon water in a small bowl and mix well.

2 Heat a wok over high heat, add the oil and swirl to coat the sides. Add the garlic, spring onion and chilli, and stir-fry for 1 minute, or until fragrant. Add the chicken and cook for 3 minutes, or until lightly browned.

3 Add the snow peas and the fish sauce mixture to the pan and scrape off any sediment from the bottom of the wok. Reduce the heat and simmer for 2 minutes, or until the tomato is soft and the chicken is cooked through. Serve immediately with steamed rice.

NUTRITION PER SERVE
Protein 57 g; Fat 20 g; Carbohydrate 10 g; Dietary Fibre 6.5 g; Cholesterol 110 mg; 1887 kJ (450 cal)

Mix together the fish sauce, lime juice, tomato, basil and water.

Add the chicken to the wok and stir-fry until lightly browned.

Simmer until the tomato is soft and the chicken is cooked through.

BEEF AND BLACK BEAN SAUCE WITH NOODLES

Preparation time: 15 minutes
Total cooking time: 10 minutes
Serves 1

70 g instant noodles
125 g beef, thinly sliced
1 teaspoon sesame oil
1 clove garlic, crushed
1 teaspoon grated fresh ginger
2 teaspoons oil
1 spring onion, sliced on the diagonal
1/4 small red capsicum, thinly sliced
4 snow peas, halved on the diagonal
1 tablespoon black bean and garlic sauce (see Note)
1 tablespoon hoisin sauce
1/4 cup (25 g) bean sprouts

1 Cook the noodles according to the manufacturer's directions, then drain and keep warm.
2 Place the beef, sesame oil, garlic and ginger in a bowl and mix together well. Heat 1 teaspoon of the oil in a wok over high heat. Add the beef mixture and stir-fry for 2–3 minutes, or until the beef is just cooked. Remove from the wok.
3 Add the remaining oil to the wok. Add the spring onion, capsicum and snow peas and stir-fry for 2 minutes. Return the beef to the wok and stir in the black bean and garlic sauce, hoisin sauce and 1 tablespoon water.
4 Add the noodles to the wok and stir through to heat and coat with the beef and vegetables. Serve immediately, topped with bean sprouts.

NUTRITION PER SERVE
Protein 30 g; Fat 20 g; Carbohydrate 25 g; Dietary Fibre 5.7 g; Cholesterol 76 mg; 1751 kJ (418 cal)

COOK'S FILE

Note: Black bean and garlic sauce is available at Asian grocery stores or in the Asian section of good supermarkets.

Add the beef mixture to the wok and stir-fry over high heat.

Stir-fry the spring onion, capsicum and snow peas for 2 minutes.

Add the noodles and stir to coat with the beef and vegetables.

CHICKEN WITH SOY AND HOKKIEN NOODLES

Preparation time: 10 minutes +
 10 minutes standing
Total cooking time: 10 minutes
Serves 1

150 g Hokkien noodles
2 teaspoons oil
150 g chicken thigh fillet, trimmed and sliced
1 small clove garlic, chopped
2 cm piece fresh ginger, julienned
1 spring onion, sliced on the diagonal
1/2 carrot, finely sliced on the diagonal
100 g broccoli, cut into small florets
1 tablespoon mirin
2 tablespoons soy sauce
1/2 teaspoon soft brown sugar
1 tablespoon toasted sesame seeds

1 Place the noodles in a bowl, cover with boiling water and leave for 10 minutes, or until tender.

2 Meanwhile, heat a wok over high heat, add the oil and swirl to coat the sides. Add the chicken and stir-fry for 5 minutes, then add the garlic and ginger and cook for 1 minute, or until fragrant. Add the spring onion, carrot and broccoli and cook for 4–5 minutes, or until the vegetables are tender.

3 Mix together the mirin, soy sauce and sugar and stir into the chicken mixture. Drain the noodles, add to the wok and cook until heated through. Serve sprinkled with the sesame seeds.

NUTRITION PER SERVE
Protein 64 g; Fat 25 g; Carbohydrate 114 g; Dietary Fibre 12 g; Cholesterol 100 mg; 3930 kJ (939 cal)

Add the garlic and ginger to the chicken and stir-fry for a further minute.

Add the spring onion, carrot and broccoli to the wok and cook until tender.

Drain the noodles, add to the wok and cook until heated through.

FRIED TOFU, CHOY SUM AND BABY CORN IN OYSTER SAUCE

Preparation time: 5 minutes
Total cooking time: 6 minutes
Serves 1

2 teaspoons peanut oil
100 g fried tofu puffs, halved
2 tablespoons oyster sauce
1 tablespoon light soy sauce

1 tablespoon sweet chilli sauce
1 tablespoon honey
1 clove garlic, crushed
4 baby corn, halved
   lengthways
4 choy sum leaves, cut into
   10 cm lengths

1 Heat a wok over high heat, add the oil and swirl to coat the sides. Add the tofu puffs and stir-fry for 2 minutes, or until crispy and golden.
2 Place the oyster sauce, soy sauce, sweet chilli sauce and honey in a small bowl and mix together well.
3 Add the garlic, baby corn and choy sum to the wok and pour in the combined sauce, along with 1/4 cup (60 ml) water. Stir-fry for 3–4 minutes, or until the leaves have just wilted. Serve immediately with steamed rice.

NUTRITION PER SERVE
Protein 12 g; Fat 22 g; Carbohydrate 45 g; Dietary Fibre 8 g; Cholesterol 0 mg; 1975 kJ (470 cal)

Stir-fry the tofu puffs for 2 minutes, or until crispy and golden.

Place the sauces and honey in a small bowl and mix together well.

Add the garlic, baby corn and choy sum to the wok and stir-fry.

CURRIES, ONE-POTS AND BAKES

RED VEGETABLE CURRY

Preparation time: 10 minutes
Total cooking time: 22 minutes
Serves 1

1 teaspoon peanut oil
4 broccoli florets, quartered
4 cauliflower florets,
    quartered
150 g orange sweet potato,
    cut into even-size chunks
2 teaspoons red curry paste
2 x 140 ml cans coconut milk
1 teaspoon lime juice
1 teaspoon fish sauce, optional
1 tablespoon chopped fresh
    coriander

1 Heat a wok over high heat, add the oil and swirl to coat the sides. Add the broccoli, cauliflower and sweet potato and stir-fry for 3 minutes. Pour 1/4 cup (60 ml) water into the wok and cover. Reduce the heat to low and steam the vegetables for 8–10 minutes, or until cooked but still crunchy.

2 Remove the lid and stir through the curry paste. Cook over medium heat for 30 seconds, or until fragrant, making sure it is well combined. Remove any lumps. Stir in the coconut milk and combine well, then reduce the heat and simmer for 8 minutes, or until slightly thickened.

3 Stir in the lime juice and fish sauce and sprinkle with the coriander. Serve immediately with rice.

NUTRITION PER SERVE
Protein 22 g; Fat 63 g; Carbohydrate 40 g; Dietary Fibre 18 g; Cholesterol 0.5 mg; 3434 kJ (820 cal)

COOK'S FILE

Note: Different curry pastes, such as green or Panang, will alter the flavour.

Steam the vegetables in the wok until cooked but still crunchy.

Add the coconut milk to the wok and simmer until slightly thickened.

GREEN CHICKEN CURRY

Preparation time: 10 minutes
Total cooking time: 5 minutes
Serves 1

1 teaspoon peanut oil
2 teaspoons green
   curry paste
1 chicken thigh fillet,
   thinly sliced
140 ml can coconut milk
4 broccoli florets, halved
4 green beans, cut into
   4 cm lengths
1/4 cup (7 g) fresh
   coriander leaves
2 teaspoons fish sauce
fresh coriander leaves,
   extra, to garnish
shredded fresh kaffir lime
   leaves, to garnish

1 Heat a wok over high heat, add the oil and swirl to coat the sides. Add the curry paste and the chicken and stir-fry for 1 minute, or until the chicken is lightly browned.

2 Reduce the heat to low and add the coconut milk and broccoli. Cook, stirring constantly, for 2 minutes, then add the green beans and cook for a further 2 minutes.

3 Remove the wok from the heat and stir in the coriander leaves and fish sauce. Top with the extra coriander leaves and the shredded kaffir lime leaves and serve immediately with steamed rice.

NUTRITION PER SERVE
Protein 45 g; Fat 40 g; Carbohydrate 7 g; Dietary Fibre 10 g; Cholesterol 75 mg; 2295 kJ (548 cal)

Use a sharp knife to finely shred the fresh kaffir lime leaves.

Add the curry paste and chicken to the wok and stir-fry for 1 minute.

Reduce the heat and add the coconut milk and broccoli, and then the green beans.

BEEF AND PINEAPPLE CURRY

Preparation time: 10 minutes
Total cooking time: 12 minutes
Serves 1

1 tablespoon peanut oil
175 g rump steak, thinly sliced across the grain
2 teaspoons Panang curry paste
1/2 small onion, cut into thin wedges
1 small clove garlic, crushed
140 ml can coconut milk
4 small kaffir lime leaves

1/2 cup (80 g) chopped fresh pineapple
1/2 teaspoon soft brown sugar
2 teaspoons lime juice
1 teaspoon fish sauce
1 tablespoon chopped fresh coriander leaves

1 Heat a wok over high heat, add half the oil and swirl to coat the sides. Add the beef, in batches, and stir-fry for 2 minutes, or until browned. Remove.
2 Heat the remaining oil in the wok over high heat, add the curry paste and cook for 1 minute, or until fragrant. Add the onion and garlic and cook for 1–2 minutes, or until the onion is soft.

3 Return the beef to the wok, add the coconut milk, lime leaves and pineapple and bring to the boil, then reduce the heat and simmer for 5 minutes, or until the beef is just cooked. Stir in the remaining ingredients and serve with steamed jasmine rice.

NUTRITION PER SERVE
Protein 47 g; Fat 53 g; Carbohydrate 23 g; Dietary Fibre 7 g; Cholesterol 118 mg; 3137 kJ (749 cal)

COOK'S FILE

Note: Any curry paste can be used if Panang curry paste is not available, however, the flavour will be different.

Stir-fry the beef in batches over high heat until browned.

Add the onion and garlic and cook until the onion is soft.

Stir in the coconut milk, lime leaves and pineapple and simmer for 5 minutes.

SPINACH RICOTTA BAKE

Preparation time: 10 minutes
Total cooking time: 20 minutes
Serves 1

**1 thin slice processed leg ham
100 g English spinach leaves
150 g ricotta
3 tablespoons grated Parmesan
pinch ground nutmeg
2 egg whites**

1 Preheat the oven to hot 220°C (425°F/Gas 7). Lightly grease a 1 1/2 cup (375 ml) soufflé or ovenproof dish and line the base and side of the dish with the ham. The ham should not overlap the sides.
2 Place the spinach in a steamer and steam for 4–5 minutes, or until wilted. Drain, squeeze out any excess liquid and chop. Mix together the spinach, ricotta and half the Parmesan and season with salt, pepper and nutmeg.
3 Place the egg whites in a small, dry bowl and whisk with electric beaters

until soft peaks form. Gently fold into the spinach mixture. Spoon into the prepared dish and sprinkle with the remaining Parmesan.
4 Bake for 15 minutes, or until risen and golden brown. Run a sharp knife around the inside of the dish and turn the bake out. Serve ham-side-down with a tossed salad.

NUTRITION PER SERVE
Protein 40 g; Fat 28 g; Carbohydrate 2.5 g; Dietary Fibre 2.5 g; Cholesterol 112 mg; 1768 kJ (422 cal)

Line the soufflé or ovenproof dish with the slice of ham.

Place the spinach, ricotta and half the Parmesan in a bowl, season and mix well.

Gently fold the egg whites into the spinach mixture.

FENNEL AND MUSHROOM GRATIN

Preparation time: 5 minutes
Total cooking time: 20 minutes
Serves 1

1 small potato
1 large fennel bulb
10 g butter
2 teaspoons olive oil
1 small clove garlic, crushed
50 g button mushrooms, sliced
1 tablespoon white wine or dry
   vermouth
1/4 cup (60 ml) cream

1 teaspoon chopped fresh thyme
30 g semi-dried tomatoes,
   chopped
2 tablespoons grated Parmesan

1 Bring a small saucepan of salted water to the boil, add the potato and boil for 5 minutes, or until tender. Cool, then cut into 5 mm slices.
2 Meanwhile, lightly grease a 2 cup (500 ml) shallow ovenproof dish. Cut the top and base off the fennel and remove any tough outer layers. Thinly slice the fennel.
3 Heat the butter and oil in a frying pan, add the fennel and cook over low heat for 6 minutes, or until soft. Add

the garlic and mushrooms and cook for a further 6 minutes. Add the wine, cream, thyme and tomato, reduce the heat and simmer for 2 minutes, stirring occasionally. Stir in 1 tablespoon of the grated Parmesan.
4 Place the fennel mixture in the prepared dish, layering it with the potato. Sprinkle with the remaining Parmesan and place under a hot grill for 1–2 minutes, or until the cheese melts. Serve with a tossed green salad.

NUTRITION PER SERVE
Protein 18 g; Fat 50 g; Carbohydrate 17 g; Dietary Fibre 6.5 g; Cholesterol 136 mg; 2504 kJ (600 cal)

Trim the fennel, remove any tough outer layers and thinly slice.

Add the garlic and mushrooms to the fennel and cook for 6 minutes.

Place the fennel mixture in the prepared dish, layering it with the potato slices.

LAMB MOUSSAKA

Preparation time: 20 minutes
Total cooking time: 45 minutes
Serves 1

1 small eggplant
2¹/₂ tablespoons olive oil
1 clove garlic, crushed
1 small onion, finely sliced
200 g lamb mince
2 tablespoons white wine
2 teaspoons tomato paste
1 tomato, chopped
2 teaspoons chopped fresh
    flat-leaf parsley
¹/₂ teaspoon chopped
    fresh mint
pinch ground cinnamon

Cheese sauce
10 g butter
2 teaspoons plain flour
¹/₂ cup (125 ml) milk
1 tablespoon grated Romano
    cheese
1 tablespoon grated Cheddar

1 Preheat the oven to moderately hot 200°C (400°F/Gas 6). Lightly grease a 2 cup (500 ml) baking dish.
2 Cut two 1 cm thick slices from the eggplant. Heat 2 tablespoons of the oil in a small frying pan and cook the eggplant slices for 2–3 minutes on each side, or until golden.
3 Heat the remaining oil in a small saucepan, add the garlic and onion and cook over low heat for 2 minutes, or until soft. Increase the heat to medium, add the mince and cook for 5 minutes, or until browned. Add the white wine, tomato paste, tomato, parsley, mint and cinnamon. Reduce the heat to low and cook, covered, for

10 minutes. Season and leave to cool.
4 To make the sauce, melt the butter in a small saucepan and stir in the flour. Cook for 1 minute, or until it starts to change colour. Remove from heat and slowly add the milk, stirring until smooth. Return to the heat, bring to the boil, add the cheeses and stir until thick and smooth. Season with salt and freshly ground black pepper.
5 Place one of the eggplant slices on the bottom of the baking dish, top

with half the lamb mixture, repeat with the remaining eggplant slice and the lamb, then pour the cheese sauce over the top and smooth over to cover.
6 Place in the oven and bake for 15–20 minutes, or until lightly browned on top. Serve with a green salad.

NUTRITION PER SERVE
Protein 60 g; Fat 78 g; Carbohydrate 20 g; Dietary Fibre 7.5 g; Cholesterol 200 mg; 4405 kJ (1052 cal)

Cook the eggplant in a frying pan until golden on each side.

Add the white wine, tomato paste, tomato, parsley, mint and cinnamon.

Pour the cheese sauce over the top of the lamb mixture.

MIDDLE EASTERN POTATO CASSEROLE

Preparation time: 10 minutes
Total cooking time: 30 minutes
Serves 1

300 g potatoes, cut into large
   cubes
1 teaspoon olive oil
1 small onion, sliced
1/2 teaspoon ground turmeric
1/2 teaspoon ground coriander
1 cup (250 ml) vegetable stock
1 clove garlic, crushed

1/4 teaspoon saffron threads,
   soaked in 1 tablespoon
   hot water
1/4 cup (30 g) raisins
1 teaspoon chopped fresh
   flat-leaf parsley
1 teaspoon chopped fresh
   coriander leaves

1 Place the potato in a saucepan of cold, salted water. Bring to the boil and cook until the potato is tender but still firm, as it will be cooked further. Drain and set aside.
2 Heat the oil in a separate saucepan, add the onion, turmeric and ground coriander and cook over low heat for 5 minutes, or until the onion is soft.
3 Add the potato, vegetable stock and garlic. Bring to the boil, then reduce the heat and simmer for 10 minutes.
4 Add the saffron, and soaking water, and raisins, and cook for 10 minutes, or until the potato is soft and the sauce has reduced and thickened. Stir in the parsley and coriander. Serve with couscous.

NUTRITION PER SERVE
Protein 10 g; Fat 6 g; Carbohydrate 65 g;
Dietary Fibre 8 g; Cholesterol 0.5 mg;
1500 kJ (358 cal)

Soak the saffron threads in 1 tablespoon hot water.

Cook the onion, turmeric and ground coriander until the onion is soft.

Add the potato, stock and garlic to the saucepan and bring to the boil.

MINI COTTAGE PIE

Preparation time: 15 minutes
Total cooking time: 45 minutes
Serves 1

1 teaspoon oil
1/4 small onion, finely chopped
1/4 carrot (20 g), finely chopped
1 clove garlic, crushed
200 g minced beef
2 1/2 teaspoons plain flour
1 1/2 cups (375 ml) beef stock
2 teaspoons tomato paste
2 teaspoons Worcestershire
   sauce
1 large (300 g) potato,
   cut into small chunks
3 teaspoons milk
15 g butter

1 Preheat the oven to moderately hot 200°C (400°F/Gas 6). Lightly grease a 2 cup (500 ml) ovenproof dish.

2 Heat the oil in a deep frying pan, add the onion and carrot and cook for 2 minutes, or until the onion is soft. Add the garlic and minced beef and cook for 3–4 minutes, or until the meat is browned. Sprinkle on the flour and stir through. Gradually add the stock, stirring until smooth. Add the tomato paste and Worcestershire sauce, bring to the boil, then reduce the heat and simmer for 15 minutes, or until reduced. Remove from the heat and season with salt and freshly ground black pepper.

3 To make the potato topping, bring a small saucepan of water to the boil, add the potato and cook for 8 minutes, or until tender. Drain well and mash with a potato masher or fork. Add the milk and butter and season with salt and freshly ground black pepper. Mix until smooth and fluffy.

4 Spoon the meat mixture into the prepared ovenproof dish and then spread the potato topping evenly over the top, roughing up the surface with a fork. Bake for 12–15 minutes, or until heated through. Place under a hot grill to brown and crisp the topping, if desired.

NUTRITION PER SERVE
Protein 50 g; Fat 40 g; Carbohydrate 50 g; Dietary Fibre 7 g; Cholesterol 167 mg; 3195 kJ (763 cal)

Once the meat is browned, sprinkle on the flour and stir in well.

Simmer the mixture for 15 minutes, or until reduced.

Cook the potato chunks in boiling water for 8 minutes, or until tender.

Rough up the surface of the potato topping with a fork.

CORNISH PASTIES

Preparation time: 20 minutes
Total cooking time: 35 minutes
Makes 2 pasties

75 g beef mince
1/4 small onion, finely chopped
**2 tablespoons finely diced
  potato**
**2 tablespoons finely diced
  turnip**
**2 tablespoons finely diced
  carrot**
**1 teaspoon finely chopped fresh
  flat-leaf parsley**
2 sheets puff pastry
1 egg, lightly beaten

1 Preheat the oven to hot 210°C (415°F/Gas 6–7). Place the beef, onion, potato, turnip, carrot and parsley in a bowl, mix well and season with salt and freshly ground black pepper.
2 Cut the puff pastry sheets into two 17 cm circles. Place half the filling in the centre of each and lightly brush the edges of the pastry with a little water. Bring the edges together so the seam is in the centre and press to seal, folding the edge to form a pattern.
3 Prick the pastry with a fork, brush with the egg and place on a lined baking tray. Bake for 10 minutes, then reduce the oven temperature to moderately hot 190°C (375°F/Gas 5), and cook for 25 minutes, or until golden brown. Serve the pasties with tomato sauce, if desired.

NUTRITION PER PASTIE
Protein 21 g; Fat 45 g; Carbohydrate 65 g; Dietary Fibre 4 g; Cholesterol 156 mg; 3116 kJ (745 cal)

Place the beef, onion, potato, turnip, carrot and parsley in a bowl and mix well.

Place half the filling in the centre of each pastry circle and bring the edges together.

Reduce the heat and cook the pasties for 25 minutes, or until golden brown.

COOKING TO FREEZE

PORK AND VEAL RISSOLES

Preparation time: 20 minutes
Total cooking time: 15 minutes
Makes 4 serves

800 g pork and veal mince
1 1/2 cups (120 g) fresh
    breadcrumbs
1 egg, lightly beaten
2 teaspoons chopped fresh thyme
3 tablespoons fruit chutney
1 clove garlic, crushed
8 thin rashers bacon, cut in
    half lengthways
8 sprigs fresh thyme

1 Place the mince, breadcrumbs, egg, thyme, chutney and garlic in a large bowl. Season and mix with your hands. Divide the mixture into 8 even portions and form into patty shapes.

2 Wrap a length of bacon around one patty and then another length around in the other direction. Secure with a toothpick. Tuck a sprig of thyme under the centre of the bacon cross. Repeat with the remaining patties.
3 Place the patties on a baking tray covered with baking paper and freeze until just firm. When firm, wrap the patties in plastic wrap and place in a freezer bag or airtight container and freeze for up to 3 months.
4 To cook, thaw two patties in the refrigerator. Heat a lightly greased frying pan, add the patties and cook over medium heat for about 6 minutes each side, or until well browned and cooked through. Serve with potato wedges and steamed vegetables.

NUTRITION PER SERVE
Protein 65 g; Fat 9 g; Carbohydrate 22 g; Dietary Fibre 1.5 g; Cholesterol 182 mg; 1825 kJ (436 cal)

Wrap two strips of bacon around each rissole and secure with a toothpick.

Cook the patties in a lightly greased frying pan until cooked through.

CHICKEN AND VEGETABLE SOUP

Preparation time: 20 minutes
Total cooking time: 30 minutes
Makes 4 serves

2 teaspoons oil
1 small onion, finely chopped
1 stick celery, finely chopped
1 small carrot, grated
1 small potato, grated
1.5 litres chicken stock
2 small chicken breast fillets,
   cut into small pieces

75 g green beans, cut into
   1 cm lengths
1 small zucchini, diced
1/4 cup (35 g) frozen baby peas
1/4 cup (7 g) finely chopped
   fresh flat-leaf parsley

1 Heat the oil in a large saucepan. Add the onion and celery and cook, stirring, for 2–3 minutes, or until soft. Add the carrot, potato and stock. Bring slowly to the boil, stirring.

2 Reduce the heat, add the chicken and simmer for 20 minutes, stirring occasionally. Remove any scum that forms on the surface.

3 Add the beans, zucchini and peas and simmer for a further 5 minutes, or until the vegetables are just tender but still crisp. Stir in the parsley and season with freshly ground black pepper. Cool, then divide into four portions and freeze in snap-lock bags or airtight containers for up to 3 months. Defrost in the fridge or microwave and reheat gently in a saucepan over medium heat.

NUTRITION PER SERVE
Protein 14 g; Fat 4 g; Carbohydrate 7 g; Dietary Fibre 2.5 g; Cholesterol 25 mg; 490 kJ (117 cal)

Remove any scum from the surface with a skimmer or slotted spoon.

Add the beans, zucchini and peas and simmer until just tender.

Cool, then divide into four portions for freezing.

CHICKEN WITH TOMATOES, OLIVES AND CAPERS

Preparation time: 20 minutes
Total cooking time: 1 hour
Makes 4 serves

2 tablespoons olive oil
1 red onion, cut into thin wedges
1 stick celery, sliced
150 g cap mushrooms, thickly sliced
3–4 cloves garlic, thinly sliced
8 chicken thigh cutlets, skin and fat removed
plain flour, for dusting
1/2 cup (125 ml) white wine
300 ml chicken stock
400 g can chopped tomatoes
1 tablespoon tomato paste
1/3 cup (60 g) black olives
1 tablespoon capers

1 Heat half the oil in a large non-stick frying pan. Add the onion, celery, mushrooms and garlic and cook, stirring, for 5 minutes, or until the onion is soft. Remove from the pan.
2 Coat the chicken lightly in flour, shaking off any excess. Heat the remaining oil in the frying pan and cook the chicken, in batches, turning once, for 5 minutes, or until well browned. Add the wine and stock and cook for a further 2 minutes.
3 Return the cooked vegetables to the pan and add the tomato and tomato paste. Simmer, partially covered, for 40 minutes, or until the sauce has reduced slightly. Uncover during the last 10 minutes if the sauce has not reduced enough. Add the olives and capers and season with black pepper. Cool and divide into four portions.

Place in airtight containers and freeze for up to 3 months. To reheat, defrost and gently reheat in a microwave or saucepan. Serve with pasta or rice.

NUTRITION PER SERVE
Protein 11 g; Fat 11 g; Carbohydrate 11 g; Dietary Fibre 4.3 g; Cholesterol 14 mg; 874 kJ (210 cal)

Cook the onion, celery, mushrooms and garlic in a frying pan.

Cook the chicken, turning once, until well browned all over.

Add the tomato and tomato paste to the pan and simmer for 40 minutes.

VEGETARIAN LASAGNE

Preparation time: 20 minutes
Total cooking time: 40 minutes
Makes 4 lasagnes

250 g packet instant lasagne
    sheets
1 tablespoon olive oil
2 cloves garlic, crushed
2 x 400 g cans diced tomatoes
1 tablespoon tomato paste
1 teaspoon soft brown sugar
200 g semi-dried tomatoes,
    chopped
1 cup (50 g) fresh basil leaves
50 g baby English spinach
    leaves
600 g low-fat ricotta, softened
1 cup (125 g) grated
    Cheddar

1 Lightly grease four 11 cm square ovenproof dishes. Cut twelve 11 cm squares from the lasagne sheets and cook, in batches, in a large saucepan of boiling salted water for 1 minute, or until *al dente*. Place on a lightly oiled board to prevent sticking.

2 Heat the oil in a saucepan over medium heat, add the garlic and cook for 1 minute, or until fragrant. Add the tomato, tomato paste, sugar, semi-dried tomato and basil leaves and simmer for 10–15 minutes, or until the mixture has slightly reduced.

3 To assemble, lay a piece of lasagne on the base of each dish and spread with half the tomato mixture. Place a second piece of pasta over the top and spread with the remaining tomato mixture. Cover with the spinach leaves and top with the remaining pasta sheet. Spread with the ricotta and sprinkle the grated Cheddar over the top. Cover each dish with plastic wrap, then cover with foil and label. Freeze for up to 3 months. To serve, defrost and preheat the oven to moderately hot 200°C (400°F/Gas 6). Bake for 20 minutes, or until the cheese is melted and golden. Serve with salad or steamed vegetables.

NUTRITION PER LASAGNE
Protein 33 g; Fat 30 g; Carbohydrate 55 g; Dietary Fibre 7 g; Cholesterol 95 mg; 2620 kJ (626 cal)

Cook the lasagne sheets in boiling salted water until al dente.

Simmer the tomato and basil mixture until slightly reduced.

Cover the tomato mixture with baby English spinach leaves.

Cover each of the four dishes tightly with plastic wrap.

CREAMY BEEF AND MUSHROOM PIES

Preparation time: 10 minutes +
30 minutes refrigeration
Total cooking time: 45 minutes
Makes 4 pies

1 tablespoon oil
400 g rump steak, cut into
2 cm cubes
1 onion, chopped
250 g button mushrooms,
sliced
3 cloves garlic, crushed
2 tablespoons plain flour
1 cup (250 ml) beef stock
1/3 cup (90 g) tomato paste
1/3 cup (90 g) light sour cream
4 sheets ready-rolled
puff pastry
1 egg, lightly beaten

1 Heat the oil in a large frying pan, add the beef and cook for 5 minutes, or until well browned. Add the onion, mushrooms and garlic and cook for 2–3 minutes, or until the onion is soft. Sprinkle on the flour and cook, stirring, for 1 minute, or until well combined. Gradually add the stock, stirring well. Stir in the tomato paste and bring to the boil, then reduce the heat and simmer for 3 minutes, or until the sauce thickens slightly. Stir in the sour cream, remove from the heat and leave to cool.

2 Grease four 9 cm round pie tins. Cut one 16 cm diameter circle and one 12.5 cm diameter circle from each sheet of pastry. Place the larger pastry rounds into the pie tins and trim any excess. Refrigerate the pastry-lined tins and the remaining pastry circles for 30 minutes.

3 Divide the cooled meat mixture among the pie dishes. Brush the rims of the pies with the beaten egg, place the smaller pastry rounds over to cover and press the edges to seal. Decorate with the prongs of a fork. Make a few slits in the pie tops to allow the steam to escape when cooking. Wrap each pie individually in plastic wrap and then in foil to seal. Label and freeze for up to 3 months.

4 To serve, remove a pie from the freezer and defrost. Preheat the oven to hot 220°C (425°F/Gas 7). Place a baking tray in the oven to heat. Put the pie on the hot baking tray and bake for 30 minutes, or until golden.

NUTRITION PER PIE
Protein 37 g; Fat 36 g; Carbohydrate 57 g; Dietary Fibre 5 g; Cholesterol 134 mg; 2985 kJ (710 cal)

Stir in the tomato paste, bring to the boil, then reduce the heat and simmer.

Gently fit the larger pastry rounds into the tins and trim any excess.

Top with the smaller pastry rounds and press the edges to seal.

CHICKEN STEW WITH WHITE BEANS AND ZUCCHINI

Preparation time: 15 minutes
Total cooking time: 1 hour
Makes 4 serves

1 tablespoon olive oil
8 chicken thigh cutlets, trimmed
1 onion, halved, thinly sliced
4 cloves garlic, finely chopped
1/4 cup (60 ml) white wine
1 cup (250 ml) chicken stock
1 tablespoon finely chopped
   fresh rosemary
1 teaspoon grated lemon rind
1 bay leaf

2 x 400 g cans cannellini beans,
   rinsed and drained
3 zucchini, halved lengthways,
   cut on the diagonal

1 Heat the oil in a large flameproof casserole dish. Add the chicken, in batches, and cook for 4 minutes each side, or until browned. Remove.
2 Add the onion to the dish and cook for 5 minutes, or until soft. Add the garlic and cook for 1 minute, or until fragrant, then add the wine and chicken stock and bring to the boil, scraping the bottom of the pan to remove any sediment.
3 Return the chicken and any juices to the pan along with the rosemary, lemon rind and bay leaf. Reduce the heat and simmer, covered, for 45 minutes, or until the chicken is tender. Stir in the cannellini beans and zucchini and divide into four portions. Place in airtight containers or snap-lock bags and freeze for up to 3 months. To serve, defrost and gently reheat in a microwave or saucepan over medium heat. Serve with rice.

NUTRITION PER SERVE
Protein 37 g; Fat 8 g; Carbohydrate 25 g; Dietary Fibre 15 g; Cholesterol 50 mg; 1394 kJ (334 cal)

COOK'S FILE

Note: The zucchini is not completely cooked before freezing as it will cook during reheating.

Brown the chicken thigh cutlets in batches in a large casserole dish.

Stir in the rinsed and drained cannellini beans and the zucchini.

Divide into four portions and place in snap-lock bags for freezing.

MEDITERRANEAN LAMB CASSEROLE

Preparation time: 15 minutes
Total cooking time: 1 hour 5 minutes
Makes 4 serves

1 tablespoon olive oil
750 g lamb from the bone, diced
1 large onion, sliced
2 cloves garlic, crushed
2 carrots, chopped
2 parsnips, chopped
400 g can chopped tomatoes
2 tablespoons tomato paste
2 teaspoons chopped fresh rosemary
1/2 cup (125 ml) red wine
1 cup (250 ml) chicken stock

1 Heat the oil in large saucepan and cook the lamb, in batches, for 3–4 minutes, or until browned. Remove from the pan and keep warm. Add the onion and garlic and cook for 2–3 minutes, or until the onion is soft.

2 Return the lamb and juices to the pan. Add the remaining ingredients, bring to the boil, then reduce the heat and simmer, covered, for 50 minutes, or until the lamb is tender and the sauce has thickened. Divide into four portions, place in airtight containers or snap-lock bags and freeze for up to 3 months. To serve, defrost and gently reheat in a microwave or saucepan until warmed through.

NUTRITION PER SERVE
Protein 45 g; Fat 12 g; Carbohydrate 12 g; Dietary Fibre 4.5 g; Cholesterol 125 mg; 1517 kJ (362 cal)

COOK'S FILE

Serving suggestion: Serve with creamy polenta. To make one serve of creamy polenta, place 1 1/2 cups (185 ml) chicken stock and 1/4 cup (60 ml) water in a saucepan and bring to the boil. Add 1/4 cup (35 g) polenta, reduce the heat and simmer for 5 minutes, or until the polenta thickens. Stir in 1 teaspoon grated Parmesan and serve.
Note: Polenta is not suitable for freezing and should be made just prior to serving.

Add the onion and garlic and cook until the onion is soft.

Simmer until the lamb is tender and the sauce has thickened.

ONION AND ROAST CAPSICUM QUICHE

Preparation time: 25 minutes +
 30 minutes refrigeration
Total cooking time: 1 hour 15 minutes
Makes 4 serves

1½ cups (185 g) plain flour
125 g cold butter, chopped
1 egg yolk

Filling
2 red capsicums
25 g butter
125 g bacon, finely chopped
1 large onion, sliced
2 teaspoons sugar
½ cup (125 ml) cream
2 eggs

1 Preheat the oven to moderate 180°C (350°F/Gas 4). Lightly grease a deep 22 cm round fluted flan dish.
2 Put the flour and butter in a bowl and rub in with your fingertips until the mixture resembles breadcrumbs. Add the egg yolk and 2 tablespoons water and mix together with a flat-bladed knife to form a rough dough. Add a little more water if the dough is too dry. Turn out onto a lightly floured surface and gather together into a smooth ball. Cover with plastic wrap and refrigerate for 30 minutes.
3 Roll the pastry out between 2 sheets of baking paper, until large enough to cover the base and side of the prepared dish. Ease the pastry into the dish and trim any excess pastry from the edges with a sharp knife. Cut a sheet of greaseproof paper large enough to cover the pastry-lined dish and place in the dish. Spread a layer of rice or dried beans evenly over the paper and bake for 7 minutes, then remove the paper and rice and return the pastry to the oven for a further 8 minutes, or until lightly golden. If any air pockets form in the pastry, gently press down with a clean tea towel to remove while still hot to prevent any cracking. Cool.
4 To make the filling, cut the capsicums into large pieces. Place on a lined grill tray and cook, skin-side-up, under a hot grill for 10 minutes, or until the skin blackens and blisters. Place in a plastic bag and leave to cool. Peel away the skin and cut the flesh into thin strips.
5 Heat the butter in a frying pan and cook the bacon for 3–4 minutes, or until crispy. Add the onion and cook over low heat for 10 minutes, or until soft and golden. Add the sugar and stir through until it has completely dissolved. Spread the bacon mixture over the base of the prepared pastry shell and top with the capsicum strips.
6 Combine the cream and eggs in a bowl or jug and season. Pour over the bacon and capsicum and place on an oven tray. Bake for 30–35 minutes or until golden. Cool, remove from the tin and cut into 4 even portions. Wrap each portion in plastic wrap, then place in freezer bags or airtight containers. Freeze for up to 3 months. To serve, defrost and remove the plastic wrap from one portion. Place on a lined baking tray and bake in a moderate oven (180°C/350°F/Gas 4) for 10 minutes, or until heated through.

NUTRITION PER SERVE
Protein 18 g; Fat 50 g; Carbohydrate 42 g; Dietary Fibre 3.5 g; Cholesterol 290 mg; 2875 kJ (685 cal)

Mix together with a flat-bladed knife to form a rough dough.

Place the rolled out pastry in the prepared flan dish and trim the edges.

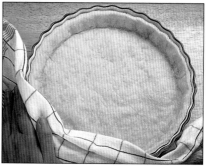

Bake the pastry in a moderate oven until lightly golden.

Peel the skin from the capsicum and slice the flesh into thin strips.

Add the sugar to the bacon and onion and stir until dissolved.

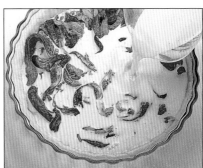

Pour the combined cream and eggs over the bacon and capsicum.

CHILLI CON CARNE

Preparation time: 10 minutes
Total cooking time: 50 minutes
Makes 4 serves

1 tablespoon olive oil
1 onion, finely chopped
3 cloves garlic, crushed
1 stick celery, chopped
500 g lean minced beef
2 teaspoons chilli powder
pinch cayenne pepper
1 teaspoon dried oregano
440 g can chopped tomatoes
2 tablespoons tomato paste

1 teaspoon soft brown sugar
1 tablespoon cider or red wine
 vinegar
420 g can red kidney beans,
 drained and rinsed

1 Heat the oil in a large saucepan, add the onion, garlic and celery and cook, stirring, over medium heat for 5 minutes, or until soft. Add the beef and cook over high heat for 5 minutes, or until well browned, breaking up any lumps with the back of a spoon.

2 Add the chilli powder, cayenne pepper and oregano to the pan and cook for 2 minutes. Add the tomato and tomato paste, and stir to mix well.

3 Reduce the heat and simmer for 30 minutes, stirring occasionally. Add the soft brown sugar, vinegar and kidney beans and season to taste with salt and freshly ground black pepper. Heat through for 5 minutes then cool. Divide into four portions, place in airtight containers or snap-lock bags and freeze for up to 3 months. To serve, defrost and gently reheat in a microwave or saucepan. Serve with sour cream, guacamole and corn chips.

NUTRITION PER SERVE
Protein 40 g; Fat 18 g; Carbohydrate 7 g; Dietary Fibre 2.5 g; Cholesterol 392 mg; 1467 kJ (350 cal)

Cook the beef until well browned, breaking up any lumps with a spoon.

Stir the tomato and tomato paste into the meat mixture.

Add the kidney beans to the saucepan and heat through.

SPICY LAMB TAGINE

Preparation time: 15 minutes
Total cooking time: 1 hour 10 minutes
Makes 4 serves

2 teaspoons ground cumin
2 teaspoons ground coriander
1 teaspoon ground ginger
1/2 teaspoon ground paprika
1/4 teaspoon ground saffron
60 g ghee or butter
1 kg boned leg lamb, diced
2 onions, chopped
3 cloves garlic, crushed
400 g can peeled tomatoes
1 1/2 cups (375 ml) chicken stock
2 tablespoons tomato paste
1 cinnamon stick
2 bay leaves
1/2 cup (90 g) dried apricots
2 zucchini, cut into 1 cm slices
1/4 cup (15 g) chopped fresh
    coriander leaves

1 Heat a frying pan over low heat and dry-fry the spices for 1 minute, or until fragrant. Do not burn.
2 Melt half the ghee or butter in a large saucepan. Add the lamb, in batches, and cook over high heat for 2–3 minutes, or until just browned. Remove from the pan.
3 In the same pan, heat the remaining ghee or butter, add the onion and garlic and cook over medium heat for 1–2 minutes, or until the onion is soft. Return the lamb to the pan and add the dry-fried spices, tomato, chicken stock, tomato paste, cinnamon stick and bay leaves and mix together well. Reduce the heat and simmer, covered, for 30 minutes.
4 Stir in the apricots, zucchini and coriander and simmer, uncovered, for

a further 30 minutes. Remove the cinnamon stick and bay leaves and season to taste. Allow to cool. Divide into four portions, place in airtight containers and freeze for up to 3 months. To reheat, defrost and gently reheat in a microwave or saucepan until warmed through. Serve with couscous or saffron rice.

NUTRITION PER SERVE
Protein 57 g; Fat 22 g; Carbohydrate 9 g; Dietary Fibre 3 g; Cholesterol 200 mg; 1940 kJ (465 cal)

Dry-fry the spices in a frying pan over low heat until fragrant.

Simmer the meat, spices, tomato, stock, tomato paste, cinnamon and bay leaves.

Remove the cinnamon stick and bay leaves prior to freezing.

LAMB SHANKS WITH TOMATO AND THYME

Preparation time: 15 minutes
Total cooking time: 2 hours
Makes 4 serves

2 tablespoons oil
4 (2 kg) lamb shanks
2 onions, finely chopped
2 cloves garlic, finely chopped
2 carrots, diced
2 sticks celery, diced
1 1/2 teaspoons dried thyme
    leaves
2 bay leaves
1/2 teaspoon paprika
2 x 400 g cans chopped
    tomatoes
1/4 cup (60 g) tomato paste
1/4 cup (60 ml) red wine
1 cup (250 ml) beef stock

1 Heat the oil in a large saucepan over high heat, add the lamb shanks, two at a time, and cook for 5 minutes, or until browned. Remove from the pan.
2 Add the onion, garlic, carrot and celery to the saucepan and cook over medium heat for 4–5 minutes, or until soft. Increase the heat to high and cook, stirring, for 10 minutes, or until slightly caramelised.
3 Add the thyme, bay leaves and paprika, and stir until aromatic. Stir in the tomato, tomato paste, wine and stock until well combined. Bring to the boil and return the lamb shanks to the pan. Cover, leaving the lid slightly ajar, reduce the heat and simmer for 1 hour 30 minutes, or until the meat falls away from the bone. Cool.
4 Divide into four portions and place in snap-lock bags or airtight containers

and freeze for up to 3 months. To serve, defrost and gently reheat in a microwave or saucepan until warmed through. Serve with potatoes or rice.

NUTRITION PER SERVE
Protein 123 g; Fat 20 g; Carbohydrate 13 g; Dietary Fibre 5.5 g; Cholesterol 330 mg; 3095 kJ (740 cal)

Cook the lamb shanks for 5 minutes, or until browned.

Cook the onion, garlic, carrot and celery until the onion is slightly caramelised.

Simmer for 1 hour 30 minutes, or until the meat falls away from the bone.

BEEF CURRY

Preparation time: 15 minutes
Total cooking time: 1 hour 35 minutes
Makes 4 serves

1 tablespoon ghee or oil
1 onion, finely chopped
2 tablespoons Madras curry
   paste
2 cloves garlic, crushed
1 kg skirt or chuck steak,
   cut into 2 cm cubes
1/4 cup (60 g) tomato paste
1 cup (250 ml) beef stock
1 teaspoon sugar

1 Heat the ghee or oil in a large saucepan, add the onion and cook for 1–2 minutes, or until soft. Add the curry paste and garlic and cook, stirring, for 1 minute, or until fragrant.
2 Add the steak to the pan and mix through until well coated with the onion mixture.
3 Stir in the tomato paste and beef stock. Bring to the boil, then reduce the heat and simmer, covered, for 1 hour 30 minutes, or until the meat is tender. Stir in the sugar. Cool and divide into four portions. Place into airtight containers or snap-lock bags and freeze for up to 3 months. To serve, defrost and gently reheat in a microwave or saucepan until warmed through. Serve with steamed rice.

NUTRITION PER SERVE
Protein 55 g; Fat 13 g; Carbohydrate 5 g; Dietary Fibre 1.5 g; Cholesterol 168 mg; 1460 kJ (350 cal)

COOK'S FILE

Note: To change the flavour of the curry, try different curry pastes.

With a sharp knife, cut the skirt or chuck steak into 2 cm cubes.

Add the steak to the saucepan and stir, coating well with the onion mixture.

Reduce the heat and simmer the curry until the meat is tender.

AFTER-DINNER TREATS

BERRY GRATIN

Preparation time: 5 minutes
Total cooking time: 5 minutes
Serves 1

**150 g fresh mixed berries
(raspberries, blueberries,
strawberries)
2 egg yolks
1 tablespoon caster sugar
3 teaspoons Grand Marnier**

1 Brush a shallow 1¹/₄ cup (315 ml) gratin or heatproof dish lightly with melted butter. Arrange the mixed berries in the dish.
2 Place the egg yolks, sugar and Grand Marnier in a small metal heatproof bowl over a pan of simmering water—the bowl should not touch the water. Whisk the mixture with electric beaters for 4 minutes, or until thick and creamy.
3 Pour over the berries and place under a hot grill for a few seconds, or until golden. Serve immediately.

NUTRITION PER SERVE
Protein 7 g; Fat 10 g; Carbohydrate 35 g; Dietary Fibre 4.5 g; Cholesterol 355 mg; 1195 kJ (285 cal)

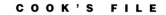

COOK'S FILE

Variation: Any combination of fresh berries can be used in this gratin. Frozen berries can also be used if fresh berries are not available. Simply defrost and pat dry with paper towels before using.
Try substituting Cointreau or fresh orange juice for the Grand Marnier. Add ¹/₄ teaspoon finely grated orange rind if using orange juice to give a bit more flavour.

Whisk the egg yolks, sugar and Grand Marnier until thick and creamy.

Pour the Grand Marnier mixture over the berries.

FLUFFY PANCAKES WITH BLUEBERRY CITRUS SAUCE

Preparation time: 10 minutes
Total cooking time: 15 minutes
Serves 1

1/4 cup (30 g) self-raising flour
1/4 teaspoon bicarbonate of soda
1 tablespoon caster sugar
1 egg yolk
10 g butter, melted
1/3 cup (80 ml) buttermilk
1 tablespoon buttermilk, extra,
    if required
5 g butter, extra
1 scoop vanilla ice cream,
    to serve

Blueberry citrus sauce
1/3 cup (50 g) blueberries,
    fresh or frozen
1 tablespoon sugar
1/3 cup (80 ml) orange juice
2 teaspoons lemon juice
1 tablespoon grated orange rind

1 Sift the flour and bicarbonate of soda into a bowl. Add the sugar and make a well in the centre. Mix together the egg yolk, butter and buttermilk in a jug, then add to the flour mixture and stir until smooth. Add an extra tablespoon of buttermilk if the mixture is too thick to pour.

2 Heat the extra butter in a non-stick frying pan over medium heat, pour one third of the mixture into the pan and cook for 2 minutes, or until bubbles form. Turn the pancake over and cook for a further minute, or until golden and cooked through. Remove and repeat with the remaining mixture to make two more pancakes.

3 To make the blueberry citrus sauce, put the blueberries, sugar, orange juice, lemon juice and half the orange rind in a small saucepan and bring to the boil. Reduce the heat and simmer for 5 minutes, or until syrupy. Stack the pancakes one on top of the other and place a scoop of ice cream on top.

Pour the sauce over the top of the pancakes and garnish with the remaining orange rind.

NUTRITION PER SERVE
Protein 11 g; Fat 18.5 g; Carbohydrate 90 g; Dietary Fibre 2 g; Cholesterol 219 mg; 2322 kJ (552 cal)

Add the buttermilk mixture to the sifted flour mixture and stir until smooth.

Pour one third of the mixture into the pan and cook until bubbles form.

Simmer the blueberry citrus sauce for 5 minutes, or until it becomes syrupy.

RICE PUDDING

Preparation time: 5 minutes +
  10 minutes soaking
Total cooking time: 1 hour 20 minutes
Serves 1

2 tablespoons medium-
  grain rice
1¼ cups (315 ml) milk

3 teaspoons caster sugar
2 teaspoons sultanas
pinch grated nutmeg

1 Preheat the oven to warm 160°C (315°F/Gas 2–3). Lightly grease a 2 cup (500 ml) ovenproof dish.
2 Place the rice in a bowl and stir in the milk and sugar. Leave for 10 minutes. Stir in the sultanas and nutmeg, then spoon into the prepared dish and bake for 1 hour 20 minutes, or until cooked through.
3 Leave for 5 minutes and remove the skin from the top of the pudding, if desired. Serve with cream or a little extra milk.

NUTRITION PER SERVE
Protein 13 g; Fat 12 g; Carbohydrate 55 g; Dietary Fibre 1 g; Cholesterol 40 mg; 1590 kJ (380 cal)

Mix together the milk, sugar and rice and leave to soak for 10 minutes.

Add the sultanas and nutmeg to the rice and milk mixture.

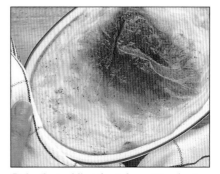

Bake the pudding for 1 hour 20 minutes, or until cooked through.

BLACKBERRY AND RASPBERRY PARFAIT

Preparation time: 5 minutes +
  20 minutes standing
Total cooking time: nil
Serves 1

45 g fresh or frozen
  blackberries
45 g fresh or frozen
  raspberries
1 tablespoon Grand Marnier
50 g coconut macaroon
  biscuits
100 g thick honey yoghurt
2 scoops vanilla ice cream

1 Combine the fresh or frozen blackberries, raspberries and Grand Marnier in a bowl and leave for 20 minutes, stirring occasionally to ensure the Grand Marnier is evenly distributed throughout the berries.
2 Put the biscuits in a plastic bag. Carefully crush with a rolling pin and then place half the biscuit mixture in the bottom of a tall glass. Add half the yoghurt, then half the berry mixture and a scoop of ice cream. Repeat the layers with the remaining biscuits, yoghurt and berry mixture, and top with another scoop of ice cream.

NUTRITION PER SERVE
Protein 9 g; Fat 19 g; Carbohydrate 56 g; Dietary Fibre 7.5 g; Cholesterol 28 mg; 1932 kJ (460 cal)

COOK'S FILE

Note: If you are using frozen blackberries or raspberries, defrost them before using. Reserve some of the defrosted berry juice and drizzle it over the ice cream just before serving.

Mix together the berries and Grand Marnier and leave for 20 minutes.

Put the biscuits in a plastic bag and carefully crush them with a rolling pin.

Add the remaining berry mixture and finish with a scoop of ice cream.

GRILLED CARDAMOM PEAR

Preparation time: 10 minutes
Total cooking time: 5 minutes
Serves 1

Honey yoghurt
1/4 cup (60 g) thick plain
    Greek-style yoghurt
1/2 teaspoon honey
1/4 teaspoon finely grated
    orange rind

1 small ripe pear, halved
    and cored (see Note)

20 g butter, melted
30 g marzipan, finely chopped
1 tablespoon soft brown sugar
1/2 teaspoon ground cardamom

1 To make the honey yoghurt, place the yoghurt, honey and orange rind in a small bowl and mix together well.
2 Place the pear halves in a shallow heatproof dish and brush with half the melted butter. Cook, rounded-side-up, under a hot grill for 2 minutes. Remove from the heat and turn over.
3 Scatter the marzipan over the pear halves. Place the sugar and cardamom in a small bowl, mix well and then sprinkle over the marzipan. Drizzle the remaining butter over the top and return the pear halves to the grill for 1 minute, or until the topping bubbles and turns golden. Serve the pear warm with a dollop of honey yoghurt.

NUTRITION PER SERVE
Protein 5 g; Fat 25 g; Carbohydrate 42 g; Dietary Fibre 1.5 g; Cholesterol 60 mg; 1665 kJ (398 cal)

COOK'S FILE

Note: To remove the core from a pear easily, swivel the tip of a teaspoon gently into each pear half.
Serving suggestion: Serve with plain or toasted sliced panettone.

Place the yoghurt, honey and orange rind in a bowl and mix well to combine.

Place the pear halves in a shallow heatproof dish and cook under a hot grill.

Scatter the marzipan over the pear and sprinkle with the sugar and cardamom.

Fabulous fast fruit desserts

Delicious, simple and fresh, fruit is the perfect after-dinner treat. If you feel like something a little more special, try one of these sensational fruit desserts.

MANGO GRANITA

Put 180 g frozen mango pieces, 2 tablespoons Sauternes and 2 teaspoons lime juice in a food processor or blender and process until smooth. Add $3/4$ cup (185 ml) water and 1 teaspoon sifted icing sugar. Pour into a shallow metal dish and freeze until beginning to freeze around the edges. Scrape back into the mixture with a fork. Repeat every 30 minutes until the mixture has oversized ice crystals. Beat with a fork and refreeze just before serving.

RUM BANANA

Cut a ripe banana in half horizontally. Melt 30 g butter in a small frying pan, add 1 tablespoon soft brown sugar and stir until all the sugar has dissolved. Add 2 tablespoons good-quality rum and 2 tablespoons cream and mix together well. Then place the banana halves in the frying pan and cook them on each side for 1–2 minutes. Place on a serving plate and drizzle with the sauce. Serve hot with ice cream.

PINEAPPLE FRENCH TOAST

Place 1 tablespoon milk, 1 egg and $1/4$ cup (60 ml) pineapple juice in a small bowl and beat together. Heat 20 g butter in a frying pan until foaming. Cut two thick slices of sweet brioche and coat each side with the milk and pineapple juice mixture, allowing a little to soak into the bread. Place in the pan and cook on each side for 2–3 minutes, or until golden brown. Serve with ice cream.

MERINGUE-COVERED FRUIT

Preheat the oven to hot 220°C (425°F/Gas 7). Cut a peach or nectarine in half and remove the stone. Place cut-side-down in a bowl, cover with boiling water, and then cold water. Drain and peel the skin away. Roll 10 g marzipan into 2 balls and put in the gaps left by the stone. Put the fruit back together and place in a shallow, ovenproof dish. Whisk 1 egg white until soft peaks form, gradually add 1/4 cup (60 g) sugar and whisk to stiff peaks. Cover the fruit with the mixture, using a fork to rough up the surface. Sprinkle with demerara sugar and bake for 15–20 minutes, or until lightly brown. Serve with cream or ice cream.

PEAR TURNOVER

Preheat the oven to moderately hot 200°C (400°F/Gas 6). Melt 10 g butter in a small frying pan and add 140 g drained canned pear pieces, 1 teaspoon soft brown sugar and a pinch of cinnamon. Cook for 2–3 minutes, or until slightly caramelised. Cut two 13.5 cm circles from a sheet of puff pastry. Place half the pear mixture in the centre of each, brush the edges with beaten egg, fold over and seal with a fork. Place on a greased baking tray, brush with beaten egg, sprinkle with sugar and bake for 20–25 minutes, or until golden. Serve with cream.

MOROCCAN ORANGE WITH PANETTONE

Put 1/4 cup (60 ml) water and 11/2 tablespoons sugar in a small saucepan. Stir over low heat until dissolved. Add 3 cardamon pods and 1/2 teaspoon orange blossom water. Mix together well, increase the heat and boil for 3–4 minutes, or until reduced and slightly thickened. Remove the pods and stir in 1 segmented orange. Slice a small panettone into 3. Heat 15 g butter in a frying pan and brown the slices for 1 minute on each side. Place on a serving plate, add the orange and liquid and top with toasted pistachio nuts.

Clockwise from top left: Mango granita; Rum banana; Pineapple French toast; Moroccan orange with panettone; Pear turnover; Meringue-covered fruit.

CHOCOLATE MOUSSE

Preparation time: 15 minutes +
  2 hours chilling
Total cooking time: 5 minutes
Serves 1

50 g dark chocolate, chopped
1/4 cup (60 ml) cream
1 egg, separated
1 egg white
2 teaspoons caster sugar
grated chocolate, to garnish

1 Place the chocolate in a heatproof bowl with 1 tablespoon of the cream. Bring a saucepan of water to the boil, then remove from the heat. Place the heatproof bowl over the saucepan, making sure the base of the bowl does not sit in the water. Stir occasionally until the chocolate has melted, then stir to gently mix the cream and chocolate together. Beat in the egg yolk with a wooden spoon.

2 Using electric beaters, beat the egg whites in a clean, dry bowl until soft peaks form. Gradually add the sugar and continue to beat for 30 seconds. Fold the egg whites into the chocolate mixture, then whip the remaining cream and fold through. Carefully spoon into a serving bowl and sprinkle with grated chocolate.

3 Refrigerate the chocolate mousse for 1–2 hours before serving.

NUTRITION PER SERVE
Protein 14 g; Fat 48 g; Carbohydrate 46 g; Dietary Fibre 1 g; Cholesterol 260 mg; 2728 kJ (650 cal)

COOK'S FILE

Note: For an even richer mousse, use good-quality Belgian chocolate.

When the chocolate has melted, stir gently to blend with the cream.

Beat the egg whites with electric beaters until soft peaks form.

Whip the remaining cream and fold into the chocolate mixture.

BREAD AND BUTTER PUDDING

Preparation time: 15 minutes
Total cooking time: 45 minutes
Serves 1

2 slices day-old bread,
    crusts removed
10 g butter, softened
1 tablespoon sultanas
1 teaspoon sugar
pinch mixed spice
1 egg, lightly beaten

1/4 teaspoon vanilla essence
1/2 cup (125 ml) milk
1 teaspoon demerara sugar

1 Preheat the oven to warm 160°C (315°F/Gas 2–3). Lightly grease a 1¼ cup (315 ml) ovenproof dish.
2 Cut 9 cm rounds from each slice of bread, or to fit the base of the dish. Spread one side lightly with butter and place in the base of the dish, buttered-side-up. Sprinkle with the sultanas, sugar and mixed spice. Place the egg, vanilla essence and milk in a bowl and mix well. Place the remaining bread round on top of the sultanas and pour over the egg mixture.
3 Place the pudding in a baking dish and fill with enough cold water to come halfway up the side of the dish. Bake for 40 minutes, or until lightly browned on top and cooked through. Sprinkle with sugar and place under a hot grill for 2–3 minutes, or until the sugar has melted.

NUTRITION PER SERVE
Protein 16 g; Fat 20 g; Carbohydrate 52 g; Dietary Fibre 2 g; Cholesterol 222 mg; 1849 kJ (442 cal)

Cut 9 cm rounds from each slice of bread, or to fit the base of the dish.

Pour the combined egg, vanilla essence and milk over the top of the pudding.

Bake for 40 minutes, or until lightly browned and cooked through.

APPLE CRUMBLE

Preparation time: 10 minutes
Total cooking time: 30 minutes
Serves 1

1 large green apple, peeled,
    cored and chopped into
    bite-size pieces
2 teaspoons sugar
pinch ground cinnamon

Crumble
1½ tablespoons plain flour
3 teaspoons rolled oats
1 tablespoon soft brown sugar

pinch ground nutmeg
15 g butter

1 Preheat the oven to moderate 180°C (350°F/Gas 4). Lightly grease a ¾ cup (185 ml) ovenproof dish.
2 Place the apple, sugar, cinnamon and ¼ cup (60 ml) water in a small saucepan and bring to the boil, then reduce the heat and simmer for 10 minutes, or until the apple is tender. Remove from the heat, drain and mash with a fork to give a chunky mixture. Spoon into the prepared dish.
3 To make the crumble, place the flour, oats, sugar and nutmeg in a small bowl and mix well. Rub in the

butter with your fingertips until the mixture resembles breadcrumbs. Sprinkle over the apple and bake for 15–20 minutes, or until the crumble is golden and crunchy. Serve with cream, ice cream or custard.

NUTRITION PER SERVE
Protein 3 g; Fat 13 g; Carbohydrate 60 g; Dietary Fibre 4 g; Cholesterol 38 mg; 1509 kJ (360 cal)

COOK'S FILE

Note: You can also use canned apple. Or try using other fruit combinations for a different taste, such as banana, pear or apricot with the apple.

Simmer the apple pieces for 10 minutes, or until tender.

Rub in the butter until the mixture resembles fine breadcrumbs.

Sprinkle the crumble over the apple and bake until golden and crunchy.

INDEX

INTERNATIONAL GLOSSARY OF INGREDIENTS

capsicum	red or green pepper	fresh coriander	fresh cilantro
eggplant	aubergine	English spinach	spinach
zucchini	courgette	snow pea	mangetout
tomato paste (Aus.)	tomato purée, double concentrate (UK)	tomato purée (Aus.)	sieved crushed tomatoes/ passata (UK)

Published by Murdoch Books®, a division of Murdoch Magazines Pty Limited, GPO Box 1203, Sydney NSW 1045.

Managing Editor: Rachel Carter **Editor:** Anna Sanders **Designer:** Norman Baptista **Food Director:** Jody Vassallo **Food Editor:** Rebecca Clancy **Recipe Development:** Rebecca Clancy, Michelle Earl, Joanne Glynn, Eva Katz, Barbara Lowery, Michaela Le Compte, Tracey Meharg, Sally Parker, Wendy Quisumbing, Margot Smithyman, Maria Villegas, Lovoni Welch **Home Economists:** Alison Adams, Michelle Earl, Michelle Lawton, Tracey Meharg, Kate Murdoch, Justine Poole, Clare Simmonds, Angela Tregonning, Maria Villegas **Photographers:** Ben Dearnley, Reg Morrison (steps) **Food Stylist:** Carolyn Fienberg **Food Preparation:** Justine Poole, Alison Adams **Nutritionist:** Thérèse Abbey **UK Consultant:** Maggi Altham.
CEO & Publisher: Anne Wilson **International Sales Director:** Mark Newman.

The nutritional information provided for each recipe does not include garnishes or accompaniments, such as rice, unless they are included in specific quantities in the ingredients list. The values are approximations and can be affected by biological and seasonal variations in food, the unknown composition of some manufactured foods and uncertainty in the dietary database. Nutrient data given are derived primarily from the NUTTAB95 database produced by the Australian New Zealand Food Authority.
National Library of Australia Cataloguing-in-Publication Data. Cooking for One. Includes index. ISBN 0 86411 917 8. 1. Cookery for one. I. Title: Family circle (Sydney, N.S.W.). 641.56 First printed 2000. Printed by Prestige Litho, Queensland. PRINTED IN AUSTRALIA.